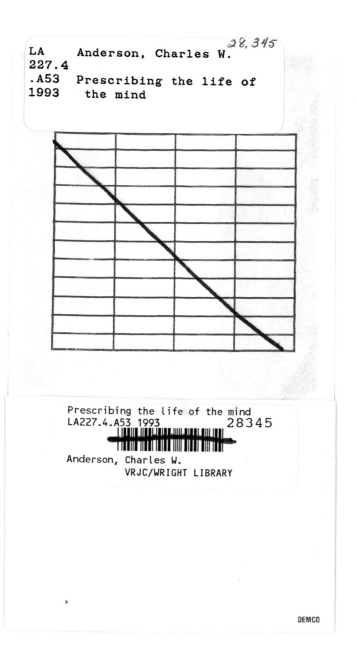

Prescribing the
Life of the Mind

Prescribing the
Life of the Mind

An Essay on the Purpose of the University,
the Aims of Liberal Education,
the Competence of Citizens,
and the Cultivation of Practical Reason

CHARLES W. ANDERSON

THE UNIVERSITY OF WISCONSIN PRESS

The University of Wisconsin Press
114 North Murray Street
Madison, Wisconsin 53715

3 Henrietta Street
London WC2E 8LU, England

Library of Congress Cataloging-in-Publication Data
Anderson, Charles W., 1934–
Prescribing the life of the mind : an essay on the purpose
of the university, the aims of liberal education, the competence
of citizens, and the cultivation of practical reason /
Charles W. Anderson.
190 p.   cm.
Includes bibliographical references (p. 261) and index.
ISBN 0–299–13830–5   ISBN 0–299–13834–8 (pbk.)
1. Education, Higher—United States—Philosophy. 2. Education,
Humanistic—United States. 3. Education, Higher—Political aspects—
United States. 4. Education, Higher—United States—Aims and
objectives. 5. Education, Higher—United States—Curricula.
I. Title.
LA227.4.A53   1993
378′.012′0973—dc20   92-45196

Contents

Preface

This book starts as a matter-of-fact effort to rethink the work of the university and the aims of liberal education. But it quickly becomes a reflection on freedom and authority, creativity and responsibility, truth and error. Once one comes to grips with the fundamental issues of education, once one asks, seriously and systematically, what we *can* and what we *ought* to teach, there is no way of avoiding—and then responding to—the big questions.

So this will be an exercise in doing epistemology, ethics, and pedagogy, among other things, without a license. I have absolutely no credentials either in philosophy or in the study of higher education. My background is in political science and political economy. I have spent most of my time thinking about the state's relationship to the productive apparatus of society. I got into this project because I wanted to apply a method of practical political reason I developed in a book named *Pragmatic Liberalism* to a concrete problem. Normally, I would have chosen to study an industry, a craft, or a profession, for I am fascinated by questions of productive technique and good practice: those moral-technical questions of the best way to make things and the right way to do things. However, for a variety of reasons, the times were not ripe for such a study, so I turned to the university, an institution which I know intimately and with which I have had a lover's quarrel for the better part of thirty years. The problem then became to look at the university as a problem in politics, defined as prescriptive choice, and in economics, defined as efficiency in pursuit of purpose and craftsmanship. And in the end, as I say, I found that these issues turned on fundamental questions of philosophy—of meaning and the world, objectivity and subjectivity, the known and the knowable.

Now many questions can be asked about the performance of the contemporary university. (I am here using the word "university" to cover all our institutions of higher education, public and private, the major research centers as well as the liberal arts and community colleges.) We still have a peculiar confidence in these institutions—and a loyalty to them. But one now senses a certain uneasiness, a vague dissatisfaction. Something is not quite right.

The more dramatic charges are probably the least important. People write grave best-sellers protesting that the universities are corrupting the young. But that old chestnut has been around since the time of Socrates. It is true now, as always, that some very strange things are taught in the universities, and we will take up the issues raised by some of these teachings in due course. But this is probably not the heart of the matter.

The more important questions probably have to do with that vague sense of disappointment experienced by students, parents, faculty, administrators, and the public at large. The university does not quite live up to our expectations. It is not quite as good as it should be. Somehow the university seems adrift, spinning its wheels, aimless. It does not seem much interested in teaching, but worse, it does not quite seem to know *what* to teach. Is a curriculum built around narrow and sometimes exotic research specialties really suited to ennoble the life of the mind or prepare people for the work of the everyday world?

My purpose then is to work through these problems and look for remedies. In the end, I will propose that we take the development of practical reason as the basis for building an integrated program of liberal education. Precisely what "practical reason" means will become apparent as we move along, for the very inquiry in which we will be engaged is designed as an exercise in practical reason.

I will argue that this conception of educational purpose better meets our expectations for the educational mission of the university, and better fits its capabilities, than any of the other options now being debated. I will also argue that this is a middle ground between identifiable extremes. Others may call for the radical transformation of higher education, or the return to a long-lost (and very hypothetical) golden age. But all of that is not really very helpful. What we have to know now is how to make the most of the materials at hand. To focus on the cultivation of practical reason as a way of integrating the curriculum is not so much to propose a new ideal of education as it is to remind us of a sense of purpose that once gave unity to our efforts. It is an ideal I believe we can recapture.

I will make some concrete proposals for the integration of the liberal arts curriculum. However, in the end it is not the plan but the philosophy that counts. And, as I have already suggested, at the heart of the matter are questions of truth—and politics.

To begin we have to come to terms with the political character of the university. The university poses a curious and perplexing, but seldom recognized, problem for the theory and practice of liberal democratic government. Liberalism, in any form, stands for freedom of thought and conscience, and for the idea that social institutions ought to reflect individual interests, not determine them. In recent years, much has been made of the point that deliberation and discussion in a liberal democratic society must not be prefigured. It must be undistorted and undominated. This is to say that, at the outset at least, all opinions count the same. Neither the force of tradition nor the judgment of the "best qualified" should set preconditions for the debate, should establish *in advance* what is sounder and wiser, what is foolish and beside the point.

Yet it is precisely the purpose of the university to set the standards of truth seeking for a society, to stipulate the rules that distinguish good sense from nonsense, truth from error, excellence from mediocrity. And it is understood that the educational function of the university is to attempt to *shape* thought and conscience, apparently in complete contradiction to liberal logic.

By what right, if any, does the university do this? There are those who *think* they know the answer. It has something to do with scientific method and rational argument. But as we shall see, the closer we look at these guarantees of knowledge, the chancier they get. We could next appeal to an ideal of academic freedom and say that the university should be open to *all* ideas, all points of view. But this cannot settle the matter. The university is not merely another forum of public opinion and debate. This is not its essential purpose and we know it. One way or another, the university has to *determine* what will and will not be taught. It has to decide what will and what will not be the privileged objects of inquiry.

This is all in the day's work for those of us who spend our lives in the university. We take our authority to prescribe a curriculum, to determine who is and who is not entitled to teach, for granted. And only against the background of a very broad and penetrating idea of liberal freedom of thought and conscience does the idea of this authority seem peculiar—and in need of justification.

To justify this power to distinguish *officially* between better and worse reason, better and worse ideas, we would have to appeal to some philosophy, some cogent system of standards. Our decisions in such matters cannot be arbitrary or self-serving. Else this is a simple arrogation of power. We have to be able to show that our decisions follow from the consistent application of principles that are peculiarly pertinent to the task at hand. And this is just the catch. For who among us would dare define the standards that ought to prevail, generally, across the university? Within our narrow specialties we may be cocksure of our ability to distinguish good work from bad. But beyond this we fear to tread. Perhaps the result is mutual trust. But it may also be the worst of all possible practical ethics—one not of mutual toleration but of mutual indifference. The rule of the modern university too often becomes: "I'll let you alone if you let me alone." Thus there may be no real check on shoddiness or carelessness, let alone malpractice or quackery. Most of the problems of higher education that need to be addressed—chaotic curriculum; teachings that are increasingly narrow and fragmented when not outright triviality, faddishness and meaninglessness; reward based on responsiveness to insular specialist elites rather than broad intellectual and educational concerns; the weird perversity of a system in which all incentives run against giving due concern to the teaching of students—follow from this lack of an overarching conception of fundamental purpose.

Even in a thoroughgoing liberal republic, the people do not expect the university to profess absolute skepticism. If we were to insist that all we could say in the end was that there were many diverse points of view and that we had no way of telling the better from the worse, the general opinion would be that we might as well close our doors and disband. In the public mind, we are *expected* to seek the truth and to teach our best approximations of it.

Thus (and there is no way I can soften the force of the assertion) to be legitimate the university must endorse some conception of truth and falsity, correctness and error, plausibility and clear mistakenness, right and wrong. And not just any theory will do. Such standards must answer to our doubts and hesitations, to our critical reservations and our skepticism. For such doubt and skepticism are themselves the most vital element in the process of quality control by which we guarantee the worth of our knowledge.

My case is not that the university *lacks* an integrating philosophy, that inquiry has become so fragmented and diverse that we can no longer agree on fundamentals. I think the philosophy we need already exists. But, I shall argue, this philosophy requires reconstruction and restatement. I think that as our work has become so specialized and so routinized we have simply lost track of the overall point of the endeavor. However, from the history and the tradition of the institution, and the norms, methods, commitments, and quandaries of our diverse disciplines, I think we can find the resources to fashion a serviceable conception of what we are trying to do.

In these pages, I will in fact lay out a specific image of how the work of the university might be integrated. I certainly do not expect to win general assent to these propositions. I would be dismayed if my case were universally endorsed as a panacea, put into practice as a general program of reform. That is not what a book like this is for. Its purpose is not to settle the issue but to set thought in motion. It is only in the presence of strong hypothesis that practical reason begins. It is only by taking exception to a particular conjecture, qualifying it, modifying it, showing why it does not apply in this case or from that perspective, that we begin the very mysterious process of groping our way toward (or trying to remember?) the exact nature of our common aims. My aim is simply to provide that conjecture, so that we may begin to deliberate on our common purposes, so that we may establish a ground from which to criticize present performance, and thus correct error and develop better ways of doing things.

Pragmatic Liberalism

As I said, I intend this study to be an application of the method of practical political reason I developed in *Pragmatic Liberalism*. (In fact, you will find that this book is promised in the last sentence of that one.)

The basic point of *Pragmatic Liberalism* is that every human enterprise has a political aspect. There is a public interest in the performance of every organized, collaborative undertaking. Participation in such purposive ventures is a public responsibility and an act of citizenship.

This means that the performance of the industries, the crafts, the professions, the arts, the sciences, and the churches is a matter of public concern. There is no strict separation of the public and the private realms. There is a public interest in every systematized practice, and in our age that runs the gamut from due process of law to standard building practice to wildlife management and wilderness preservation.

All liberals, of course, have an interest in the autonomy of the critical institutions of society. And, to be sure, in the first instance, the arena for political deliberation is *within* the enterprise. It is the first responsibility of the "citizens" of the enterprise to engage in constant scrutiny of prevailing practice, to search for better ways of carrying out the public function corporately entrusted to them. It is also their concern to assure that the political order of the enterprise, its internal system of government, is just, humane, nonarbitrary, and nonexploitative.

However, the performance of the enterprise is also a matter for public scrutiny. While liberals are rightfully skittish of anything that smacks of excessive "politicization," or state control, we the people do presume that we have the right to question the judgment of experts. Nor need we assume that the invisible hand of marketlike arrangements in every area of life will automatically make everything come out right. Thus, it is not only the role of the public to consider and critique the performance of enterprise. The public may also, on some occasions, empower the state to *enhance* the performance of these diverse organized activities, through regulation to assure that best practice is standard practice, by underwriting innovations and reforms, by universalizing access to those systems (schooling, organized medicine, social insurance, transport, energy, housing) deemed essential to a decent way of life.

In *Pragmatic Liberalism* I also suggested how political and practical reason can be melded together into a single discipline of thought and judgment. Thus fundamental liberal principles can represent qualities we would see realized in the product of the enterprise as well as serving as fundamental political ideas. There is in particular, I think, a complex web of relations among our ideas of individual freedom, efficiency, social justice, and responsiveness to individual needs and interests.

Thus, if efficiency means "fittedness to purpose," and if it implies reliability and dependability as well as serviceability, this value is understood to be closely related to the realization of individual freedom. A primary aim of liberalism is to create a rational order in which individuals can lay plans and create projects with a fair sense that they can calculate their chances for success. It is for this reason that rule of law is so important to liberals. Capricious, Kafkaesque power is a terror precisely because it turns the world into a hostile and unpredictable place. But if reliability and non-arbitrariness are a fundamental test of good law, so are they also of every human social performance. It is our ability to *count on* the legal order, scientific principles, or airline schedules, supermarkets, and surgical procedures, that makes the free life possible.

The idea of justice is closely intertwined with such ideas of efficiency and reliable performance. Liberal justice is concerned with relevant distinction. In one sense, as a principle of compensation, it implies differential reward in relation to contribution to performance. In another sense, as a principle of distribution, justice has to do with the diffusion of access to specific forms of enterprise, or with the responsiveness of enterprise to individual needs and concerns.

Thus do political and practical reason work together to provide a powerful basis for the critique and perfection of systematic ways of doing things.

The Project

It is this basic framework which is the point of departure for this analysis of the contemporary university and its theory and practice of liberal education.

The first two chapters set the stage. Here I try to get perspective on the contemporary university, an institution so familiar that we can hardly realize how extraordinary, and in many ways, how strange, it truly is. Here I consider the peculiar political character of an institution whose mission it is to prescribe the criteria of intelligent thought and action for a society. I describe the theory of practical reason which will guide our inquiry, and, in the end, become a broad model for defining the purposes of liberal education. And as a baseline for our inquiry, I try to state the case for prevailing practice. I try to capture the implicit rationale for the folkways of the contemporary university.

Then, in Chapters 3 through 5, I take up the controversy about what the university *can* and what it *ought* to teach. I take up diverse perspectives, ideologies, and points of view, asking what importance we want to assign to each and whether we want to declare any of them definitive in setting the university's purposes. I begin by considering the variety of functions that we as citizens expect the university to serve, our conception of its social role. I then contrast these ideas with the *internal* view of the university's function as an institution devoted to investigation and understanding. The next step is to survey the epistemological debate, the current controversy over what we can honestly claim to know, and thus to teach. Far more than the outsider realizes, it is here that the battle lines are drawn in the struggle to decide the program of the contemporary university. In Chapter 5, I discuss the issue of teaching: how can we evaluate whether the educational mission we have set was carried out effectively and efficiently? This, as we shall see, is a far stranger and more interesting question than it initially appears to be.

In Chapters 6 and 7, I argue for a very broad concept of practical reason as an integrating theme about which to organize a curriculum of liberal education. I try to show how this would yield a coherent conception of the *process* of education—how learning and understanding proceed from stage to stage—and also a design for coordinating and integrating the work of the diverse disciplines.

Out of all these diverse expectations and perspectives, how can we settle the question of what liberal education should entail? In the last chapter I raise the problem of who has the right to define the program of higher education, and how we would know when that authority was properly exercised and when it was abused. Finally, I discuss the question of the governance of the university, simply to note how a certain idea of its constitution follows from what has been said herein.

Throughout, I shall speak often of "our" idea of the university and what "we" expect a university to be and to do. Some readers, I understand, find this inclusive language disconcerting. Who is this "we" that is being invoked? It may seem that I am presuming general assent to propositions about which reasonable people may differ. However, I quite intentionally invoke this "we" on many occasions to suggest a mood of shared deliberation and inquiry, and a search for common ground. You, the reader, may wish to keep track of when you would be exempted from this "we." This will provide a sure sense of where, and why, you take exception to the line of argument. The device is not just literary then, but critical and analytical, essential to the method, part of the very idea of practical reason it is my purpose to define and develop.

Acknowledgments

As academic projects go, this has been a remarkably simple affair. There were no grants, consultants, or conferences. I interviewed only friends, colleagues, and people I ran into along the way, and they rarely knew it at the time. Basically, I read, thought, and wrote an essay.

Still, important acknowledgments are in order. Five remarkable friends, Booth Fowler, Adolf Gundersen, Marion Smiley, Thomas Spragens, and Catherine Zuckert, commented on the manuscript, gave greatly of themselves, their penetrating powers of mind, in criticism, encouragement, and interpretation.

At one point, I had thought it would be fitting to dedicate such a book to my teachers. I tried to make a list of those whose influence had stuck, through classes, through writings, through friendship, but the project became totally unmanageable. Still, there are two who have to be singled out, for they influenced this project directly, specifically. To write this, I had to learn a new way of philosophy and a new way of writing. Annie Dillard and Juliana Hunt taught me how to do this. Their work was on my desk, to prime the pump, throughout the exercise of writing. I hear their voices, behind mine, on nearly every page.

Allen Fitchen received the project with a warmth and understanding that touched me. He, and the entire staff of the University of Wisconsin Press, have been considerate, conscientious, and painstakingly careful throughout the production of this book.

I have always closed these acknowledgments with a tribute to Jeanie. We both know these are extraneous, that our partnership hardly depends on such solemn pronouncements. Young authors usually commend their spouses for patience and forbearance. Mature authors are simply grateful. For those of you who have followed these little public confessions of affection through the years, we are still doing fine.

Prescribing the
Life of the Mind

CHAPTER ONE

Liberal Education and Practical Reason

This is to be an essay on liberal education. I will be looking for the hard, enduring core of the curriculum, for the things that every educated person should know, and know how to do. I will be respectful of tradition but my mind is fundamentally on the future. This does not mean that I have a premonition of things to come. Nor do I have a political program to promote—if that means that I want to use education to promote a particular vision of social reform. Rather, I simply want to ask how we can best go on from here. What can we do to better prepare people to think, plan, judge, empathize, wonder, hypothesize, criticize, test, invent, and imagine? These are, I earnestly hope we can agree, the sorts of things that we actually expect the university to empower people to do.

I say the theme is liberal education. But this does not mean I will be talking mainly about what is commonly called the general education program, that array of courses that is supposed to precede specialized study. Rather, I want to think broadly about the work of the university as a whole, about what holds it together, about what comprehensible sense of central mission could conceivably integrate its diverse activities. And in fact, isn't it essential to identify the point of the overall endeavor before we decide what the "core" of the curriculum might be? This then is an effort to take stock of the work of the contemporary university. I want to examine its performance from a somewhat fresh point of view. I want to ask, critically and constructively, how that performance might be improved.

This is also to be an exercise in what I shall call practical reason. Practical reason is largely a matter of being acutely self-conscious about our ideas of the purpose of a human enterprise and about the practices we institute to achieve them. In the end, I shall argue that the method of practical reason also provides the solution to our problem—that the aims of liberal education are best defined as the cultivation of the skills of practical reason. Thus, there is a nice symmetry to the argument. This is a recursive exercise. The aim is to be as self-conscious as possible about the purposes of the institution whose task it is to be as self-conscious as possible about all forms of human endeavor.

The object of this chapter then is to give an overview of the terrain. I will lay out the plan of attack, explain the method, define some essential terms, and generally give a sense of where I am going and how I intend to get there.

Purposiveness

Every once in a while, it is essential to stand back and take a fresh look. We become accustomed to the work at hand. We get caught up in the familiar and the routine. Now the problem is to regain perspective: to ask what it is, precisely, that we are trying to do.

The habit of being very self-conscious about objectives is said to be crucial to the arts of management and government. It is also essential to the skill of any trade or craft, art or science. And it is the method of philosophy, of thought itself.

It must be the first premise of our intellectual tradition that the self-conscious and systematic deliberation of purpose is the mark of fully human activity. This is a theme that persists through the ages. On this the contending schools agree. This is the idea that unifies Aristotle's thought. This is what Kant celebrated as the capacity for moral and practical reason. This is what the American pragmatists—Peirce, Royce, James, and Dewey—underscored as the distinctive work of intelligence, of the mind.

To be fully human is to be acutely conscious of purpose. Only when we once think through our aims and objectives—when we ask probing questions about the "good" we seek, about the *telos* of our acts—do we act as humans are capable of acting. And, it is also said, it is when we *reflect* on this capacity of ours to reason about the ends we *do* seek and the ends we *should* seek that we will come to recognize our distinctive place in the creation, in the order of things.

This is the great teaching. Our ability to stand back and think through purpose is a habit of mind both commonplace and exalted. This is how we get the day's work done. This is also why we try to grasp the *point* of the universe. This capacity to *create* purposes, to *define* good and evil, excellence and error, is essential to what we call free will and moral agency. It is also what is generally meant by human dignity. It is the only evidence we have that we are, perhaps, a little different, somewhat special, in the order of the world.

The University

To reflect on purpose is the first step in the exercise of practical reason. Here I plan to apply this method to the work of the university. Thus we must begin to get our expectations in order. We must *decide* what we think the university should do. I will try to show how such a definition of purpose can be made more than a postulate or stipulation, a simple assertion, an act of will. I shall try to show how we can work up to such a conception of purpose, how we can discover it, arrive at it, through a systematic process of deliberate reason.

I will focus on the contemporary American university. This is not the only manifestation of the idea of the university, of course, but in our times it is one of the more significant and, in any event, it is the one we must come to terms with.

It is, I think, about time that we stood back and took stock of the university. We tend to take this important social institution for granted. We do not really argue its ways. It seems to me that we treat the university with unusual forbearance. The university has been relatively exempt from that ritualized contempt that Americans display toward most of their large political and economic institutions. Granted, there has always been an undercurrent of disdain for the ways of the ivory tower. Nonetheless, we have no general critical theories designed to reveal the inherent depravity of the university, as we do for corporate capitalism or bureaucratic government. There have always been discreet complaints about the more apparent bumblings and corruptions of our institutions of higher learning, but there has never been anything at all resembling a general demand for their reform.

One reason why it is so hard for us to see the university in critical perspective is that we have come to see its ways as *natural*. It has initiated us into its particular visions of reality. We have taken its habits of thought as our own. It is hard to imagine an alternative. Somehow, we have come to assume, I think, that the organization of the university rests on some logical necessity, that the order of the disciplines, the specialized fields of study, actually *reflects* the order of nature. We do not even recognize the contrivance. Rather, we suppose there *are* sciences, social sciences, and humanities in perfect triune equilibrium. And we presume that the range of the social sciences, let us say—the array that runs generally from anthropology, to economics, political science, history, psychology, and sociology—is somehow complete and exhaustive, that this is what is logically entailed in the study of the human condition.

The fact of the matter is that the American university did not arise simply through a process of social evolution. It is also, in part, the product of conscious design. When one reads the histories of these institutions in the crucial, transitional period, one discerns a very widespread vision of the reforms that were in order, the institutions that should be put in place, and the credo that should support them. Remarkably, once these foundations were set, there was little inclination to reexamine them. They have simply been taken for granted.

The American university took on settled form in the closing decades of the nineteenth century. It represented a radical break from the prevalent philosophy of higher education of the day. Granted, there were anticipations of the transformation in American experience—Jefferson's design for the University of Virginia is eerily prescient[1]—but the dominant tone was set by the liberal arts colleges. Their overriding purpose was the cultivation of Christian character. The aim of the new universities, in contrast, was the production of knowledge. Their purpose was to organize and rationalize the process of discovery, much as the new industrial corporations were rationalizing the process of production.[2]

As we shall see in detail in the next chapter, most of the distinguishing traits of the contemporary university follow from this initial conception of purpose. The organization of the curriculum into discrete research disciplines, the idea of the scholar as specialized professional, the understanding of education either as training in the methods of inquiry or as the transmission of the "fruits" of organized research, all of these elements, and many more, were inherent in the philosophy of the reconstituted university from the beginning. The university has evolved and developed through the years. It has flourished. But it would be instantly recognizable to anyone who knew it from its founding. The university has developed very much within the context of its initial framework and its initial operating assumptions. In that regard, it has become a peculiarly systematic and rationalized, and a peculiarly unreflective, institution.

Another reason it is so hard to get perspective on the university is that the philosophy and structures, the procedures and rituals, of the research university have largely become standard for the system. They are the universal model for all institutions of higher education. The liberal arts colleges no longer in general have a special role, for all their protestations to the contrary. They have simply become more intimate versions of the same thing. The tone is set by the graduate schools, themselves little differentiated, which provide a standard model of the professional research scholar and distribute it throughout the system. The former teacher-training institutions, the community colleges, the church-affiliated schools all strain to fall into line, to meet the expectations passed down to them. Only a few "experimental" colleges hold out, precariously, against the tide.[3] The very universality of the model set by the research university tends to confirm its "naturalness" and its legitimacy. To teach otherwise than is prescribed by the established organized disciplines seems vaguely suspect. It smacks of quackery.

The American university represents a radical transformation of long-standing views of the purposes of this institution, of the life of the mind, of reason itself. Again, we are probably too close to the subject for proper perspective. We take as given what was in fact an extraordinary recasting of historic predispositions.

The classic understanding was that the life of philosophy, of self-conscious reflection, was the highest of human attainments, and reserved to the very few. Even in modern times, it has normally been assumed that the capacity for reflective intelligence was rather unevenly distributed. The work of the university was taken to be essentially aristocratic. It dealt with the higher questions. It prepared the qualified for the *learned* professions. The university's role was rational speculation, and in the hierarchy of human interests this was thought to be quite remote from the concerns of everyday life.

With deliberate defiance, those who created the American university (particularly the public university, though the commitment soon spread throughout the system) simply stood this idea of reason on its head. Now it was assumed that the widespread exercise of self-conscious, critical reason was essential to *democracy*. The truly remarkable belief arose that this system of government would flourish best if citizens would generally adopt the habits of thought hitherto supposed appropriate mainly for scholars and scientists. We vastly expanded access to higher education. We presumed it a general good, like transport, or power, part of the infrastructure of the civilization.

Furthermore, it was assumed that not only the exalted subjects, but the humblest ones as well, were properly the subject of rational analysis. Thus, if we could improve philosophy, science, literature, and the arts through systematic critical analysis, we could do the same for agriculture, commerce, and home economics.

These are truly extraordinary premises on which to launch a system of higher education. This is nothing less than the full force of the Enlightenment project brought to bear on the transformation of a civilization. As we go along, we shall have to ask whether this is precisely what we have in mind. However, it is best to treat these ideas with great initial respect. I know it is fashionable to disparage "mass" education, the proliferation of the more applied sciences, and, for that matter, to lament the whole idea of a society in which rational analysis and rational order drive out folkway and custom. However, this is not my position. On the whole, I am a partisan of the ways of reasoned analysis. But the main point is that we are dealing with a truly fundamental transformation in the history of thought, in our ideas of the place of mind in the world, and it would be demeaning to simply cavil over details. Better to take exception to the entire project, or to work, with discrimination and respect, for its improvement.

As an enterprise, the American university is, of course, a remarkable success story. There is a constantly increasing demand for its product. The industry has been innovative, constantly developing more diversified and convenient services tailored for different markets, needs, and expectations. Next to the home, higher education is one of the most expensive elements in the family budget, but most reckon the investment well worth the cost. Many incur great debts and defer other satisfactions to obtain these services. In a consumer society, this is one of the most valued goods. Furthermore, the American university is one of the nation's most competitive industries in world trade. Here American quality is generally deemed superior to the foreign counterpart.

Nonetheless, it is apparent that not all is well within the university. There are clear signs that something is slipping. Some of the problems—overcrowding, frazzled indifference, a general shabbiness of deferred maintenance—are the obvious result of the prevailing mood of public penuriousness that has led to the deterioration of most basic public services in the past generation. These problems need not concern us directly here. The causes, and the solutions, are basically a matter of public will and must be worked out in the larger political process.

Our concern then is primarily with the problems that run deeper, those that are rooted in our conception of the university itself. It is true that the university often is not quite as good as it looks, and it is certainly not as good as we imagine it could be. What it stands for is not exactly what we would have it stand for. What it has to teach is often not quite what we want to learn. The way of life it represents, its internal culture, its everyday routines, are somehow not quite as noble and elevating as we had hoped for. Such disappointments and frustrations, such criticisms that emerge from a disparity between expectations and performance, must rest ultimately on an idea of the university and its purposes that is different from the university that we see in practice. It is the criticism of performance that arise from thinking differently about the purpose of the university itself, from imagining it otherwise than it presently appears, that most interest us here. For these go to the heart of the exercise of practical reason.

The Appeal to Essential Purpose

The fact is, it is impossible to think practically about the university in terms of its present program and structure alone. In order to criticize its performance, in order to say that it is not quite doing the job it is *supposed* to do, we need a concept of the university which is different from the institution we know so well. But where do we get this? We could invoke tradition or "the intentions of the founders." But this is merely a conservative strategy. We want to leave the door open, not only for the repair of decadence, but for improvement, for the possibility of something new. But for that to happen we will have to appeal to a conception of the university *that never has been realized*. How else can we say that present practice is not as good as it *could* be? At this point, we are obviously entering a realm of thought that many who work according to the dominant methods of our age will find both strange and uncomfortable. We are going to have to postulate an ideal conception of the university, a notion of its *essential* purpose, of its distinctive excellence, a prototype of its natural development, of what perfectly it should become. The positivists have already sensed the danger. A note of idealism is in the air. The scent of Plato, Aristotle, perhaps of Hegel, is all around us. But there is no other way to go on. This is what practical reason requires if it is to be possible at all.

Where indeed will such a conception of essential purpose come from? The positivist suspects that we could postulate *anything*. Any ideal conception represents no more than personal predilection. We could conjure up an infinite number of conceptions of the university with absolutely no way of adjudicating among them. Deliberation would be stalemated, argument interminable. All of this is the positivist's way of inferring that practical reason, as I have defined it, is not possible at all.

In what is to come, I will try to show that we do entertain an idea of the university sufficiently clear-cut to rule out certain possible ideas of purpose as corrupt or mistaken. I will try to show that we can at least narrow the field of possibilities by appealing to such a shared conception of inherent function. If this be idealism, then make the most of it, for I am going to try to show that we need to think this way if we are to exercise practical reason, that we can think this way successfully, and that we do it all the time.

Some might think this note of idealism incompatible with the pragmatic underpinnings of my project. The misunderstanding of philosophic pragmatism—a theory which very much influenced the American universities in their formative years—is great and general. Pragmatism, as a philosophy, is anything but the doctrine of iconoclastic relativism, or worse, brute expediency, that it is commonly supposed to be. Peirce, James, Royce, and Dewey, the last particularly in his earlier works, thought themselves to be carrying on the historic project of rationalism. They were concerned with the question of how far the mind could know the world. They assumed that our purposes guided our inquiries and thus conditioned our understanding. But they also believed that the ability of our ideas to "work well in practice," to give reliable results time and time again, in a variety of situations, was the surest guarantee that finite minds could have that we might actually be getting at the underlying order of things, gaining a glimpse of what we were intended to know and to do, in a word, of truth. Peirce, in particular, simply assumed idealism in this sense. But all the great pragmatists saw themselves in a line of descent from the likes of Plato, Aristotle, and more proximately, Hegel. As James said, pragmatism was but "a new name for some old ways of thinking."[4]

How shall we apply this notion of purpose and practical reason to the problem of the university? It will not do simply to set down a definition of the ideal aims of the university from the beginning. Like most of the elemental notions—justice, integrity—that guide our moral life, we do not have a sharply discriminating, operational definition ready at hand. Rather, we proceed by mutually intelligible intimations, affirming this, denying that, each claim suggesting an aspect of the whole that we vaguely discern but cannot readily grasp. But the *referent* of our deliberations must be some dimly sensed, not quite fully articulated, image. This is what makes reasoned argument possible. We persist in trying to persuade our antagonists that there is some crucial element of the matter at hand that their case neglects, and we proceed in the good faith that if we can show them this perceptively, if we *illuminate* them, they may change their minds. And for our own part, we presume that we may *learn* from deliberation, which is to say, we keep open, and positively, the prospect that the case we are now earnestly making we will come to recognize as inadequate, because we will see a more significant, a larger truth in the matter. (All of this is a routine part of human deliberation and argument, and all of this contemporary political science, economics, sociology, psychology, and philosophy seldom acknowledge as existing at all.)

Thus, our intimations of what we take to be the *central* or *essential* purpose of the university are implicit in our arguments about the adequacy of present practice and present performance. They appear in our *justifications* of present practice and our *criticisms* of it. To come to some conception of essential purpose that can be used as a guide to practical reason, we have to take account of the grounds of these diverse arguments, assembling the archetype of purpose out of the various claims and cases introduced in deliberation.

Of course, the ideal we come to in the course of deliberation serves as no more than a working postulate. It is a way of looking at the point of the endeavor at hand that we recommend as a better standard for judgment than the evident alternatives. But this postulate is itself, naturally, tentative and corrigible. It stands ready for further reexamination and correction based on future intimations of that always elusive conception of *what it is in fact that we are trying to accomplish.*

These deliberations never end. We can never quite know what we are after. Furthermore, we can proceed only from where we are. The referent of our critique can never be other than prevailing practice. Thus, we always proceed step by step, contrasting what exists with what we think we are actually trying to do, as we conceive that idea of purpose here and now. We work from our own disappointment, our uneasiness with things as they are, toward something we only vaguely suspect might be better.

Purposes and Standards

According to practical reason, the idea of purpose will always remain irritatingly indistinct, fuzzy, undefinable. But to make judgments, we need clear criteria, interpretable standards. The whole point is to distinguish excellence and efficiency from mistake and mediocrity. To say that something has gone right or that something has gone wrong, there has to be prior agreement on a measure of right and wrong.

The problem, of course, is that all such measures are artifices. They never quite capture the meaning of our purposes as fully as we would like. The gross national product is not the same as human well-being, and standardized test scores do not measure the quality of education. We are uneasy with our criteria. We pay for precision with an unavoidable sense that our standards are diverting us from our aims. We know that we can be trapped into pursuing the measure rather than the aim—preparing students for the test, let us say, rather than for the understanding we wish them to gain.

Clear standards are necessary to practical reason. But every system of standards is arguable. And, curiously, the only way we can argue the *utility* of our standards, their capacity to capture the distinction between good and bad performance, is in relation to that elusive idea of underlying purpose we can never quite express. We are back to that nagging, ghostly presence of an ideal again.

(If one looks closely at this point, one will see that we have reached a new level of analysis. In effect, I am now talking about how we evaluate the *exercise* of practical reason, how we decide whether we are doing well or poorly in our analysis of purpose and the means to achieve it. One might say that we have reached the level of metatheory.)

In the interdependence of purpose and criteria, practical reason is just the same as scientific reason. Science requires clear criteria (what Karl Popper called "demarcation criteria")[5] to establish the truthfulness of assertions. "Truth" in science simply means that certain conditions have been met that are essential in establishing that a statement is trustworthy, reliable, and sound.

Practical reason at first sight *seems* different from scientific reason because it deals with questions of better and worse, right and wrong. We have been taught a primitive positivist notion that scientific reason deals with facts, not values. However, of course, *internally* science is very much an evaluative enterprise. The *exercise* of scientific reason consists of taking the measure of hypotheses and experimental observations, finding out if they are supportable according to recognized standards of assertion and evidence. As I shall argue throughout, scientific reason is probably best regarded as a specific form of practical reason, that in which, given the aim of discerning patterns in natural order, one attempts to establish the accuracy of statements about the world.

The challenge then lies in specifying the relationship between standards and purpose. To justify the standards we invoke to appraise practice and performance, to show why they should be accepted as indicating excellence or error, we have to point to some underlying ultimate aim. Conversely, in laying down standards, we are giving operational form to the inchoate ideal of purpose. We are *reducing* the vague, overall conception of a project to a tight, codified statement of the conditions that must be met if we are to say that a particular exercise is good enough, or not good enough, to serve the end in view.

The whole reason for trying to state precise, interpretable standards is to create agreement. The more we can reduce the ambiguity of such measures, the easier it is to show one another that something has gone well or that something has gone wrong. Yet inevitably, and ironically, the more precise, objective, and measurable our criteria of performance, the more suspect they become as an exact articulation of purpose. Then we begin to dispute whether these "proxies" really express our aims and objectives.

Any system of standards is arguable. But this does not mean that it is arbitrary. Once again, we take exception to a stipulation of criteria because it does not seem to represent our total idea of what we are trying to achieve. For us to say that our measures are not good enough can only mean that they are corrigible, that we can think of ways to bring them closer to some conception of the ideal.

Thus, to say that all stipulations of standards are conventional (as all science measures the attributes of a phenomenon, but not the "thing in itself") is not relativism. The point that our criteria are artifices, postulates, proves not the contingency, the irrationality, the conventionality, of all our systems of ideas, but precisely the reverse. The Platonists taught the distinction between images and forms. The Aristotelians knew perfectly well the difference between essence and accident. It is not the *diversity* of our ideas, but our *capacity* to argue that some conceptions are "not good enough"—that our metatheory, our paradigm itself, is in need of improvement—that puts the everyday exercise of practical reason in touch with the larger speculations of our philosophy about the mystery of the power of reason, which always seems intent on trying to reach something just beyond our grasp.

Suppose we were trying to measure educational achievement through a standardized test. Suppose you argued that the test emphasized sheer retained knowledge over analytic ability. Would you be merely stating a personal preference, a "point of view"? Or would you be appealing to an ideal of education presumably shared generally? Would you be asserting that sheer knowledge had no place among the aims of education? Or would you be suggesting that education has a number of aims and that our proposed measure emphasized some to the neglect of others? If so, is your case not precisely a search for *dike,* as the Greeks would have put it, for right relation, balance, proportion, among a number of attributes, which is, perhaps, as close as we can come to knowing the *essence* of the enterprise of education?

But how do we know that we are not fundamentally mistaken? Perhaps we are doing no more than embroidering upon an inherited idea which we cannot escape, one which is taking us far from where, could we but see clearly, we actually want to go. Our only recourse here is to the *openness* of the general system of inquiry. It is our awareness that we might be misguided by preconception, our willingness to reexamine even fundamental assumptions, to entertain argument that we should start all over again on an entirely different tack, that is as close as we can come to guaranteeing that we are not lost in the shadows of the cave altogether. This ideal of fundamental self-consciousness or self-reflectiveness is as important in practical as it is in scientific reason. Today, it is often described as "neutral discourse" or, following the lead of Jürgen Habermas, "undistorted communication."[6]

I must be careful here, for many who embrace this ideal of absolute impartiality in deliberation do so because they deem all schemes of reason to be contingent and arbitrary. Therefore, all opinions are of equal worth and merit. None is actually closer to the truth than any other. To "prefigure" communication, to impose a system of reason on discourse, is merely an act of domination. This is the position that is generally associated with the critical theory of postmodernism. It is not the position of practical reason (or Jürgen Habermas). We shall have more to say about this in time. For the moment, it is enough to note that in practical reason discourse will be prefigured by the logic of the aims at issue, the experience behind prevailing practice, and the normative and practical constraints on action. Discourse will be "distorted" by rules of pertinence, of appropriate method, of what could count as a solution to the problem at hand and what could not. To be sure, it makes good sense to keep the door open even to challenges to first assumptions. But we do not change assumptions without good reason. There is nothing in the idea of practical reason that requires us to treat all opinions as equally valid and equally worthy of serious consideration. Those who stridently persist in the view that the central "real" aim of the university should be to produce winning football teams, or promote the views of a particular religious sect, or create patriotic fervor— even those who think that barroom brawls are "just the same" as academic disputation—do not have to be heeded, as we must heed the ones who, however awkwardly, are groping after answers to the questions at the heart of the controversy, even though, for now, they can say little more than that they found their course of study "disappointing."

The Interdisciplinary Character of Practical Reason

Every theory of practical reason, as will shortly become apparent, has to have an economic, a political, and a philosophical dimension. In appraising any theory of practical reason, we can very well ask how well these requirements are met. (Put another way, I am suggesting that these are basic criteria for testing the worth of a theory of practical reason, and I shall try to show why these tests are crucial in relation to the *purpose* of practical reason itself.) As we shall also see, these are not separate, but vitally interdependent, considerations.

This also means that practical reason is not the province of any single discipline. The creation and evaluation of theories of practical reason is, as they say, an "interdisciplinary" project. However, it should also be noted that I am going to use the terms economic, political, and philosophical in a more classical, one might say in a more *essential,* sense than is conventional in the disciplines that are normally concerned with these questions. So what the "professionals" can actually contribute to this discussion is somewhat up in the air.

The Economic Element in Practical Reason

I have said that the method of practical reason requires us to define, however provisionally, the central or essential purpose of the university. But why is this step, with all its formalist, quasi-idealist overtones, necessary at all? Why not simply decide, as Clark Kerr did in proposing the idea of the multiversity, that the university performs many diverse functions for different interests and constituencies, and let it go at that? Why put a sharp point on things? Definition is argumentative and exclusionary. As organization theorists have often pointed out,[7] people may cooperate better when purposes are left a little vague. They can agree on a common course of action for different motives and reasons.

Nonetheless, to exercise practical reason, we are going to have to have an economizing principle. At some point, we are going to have to decide to do *this* rather than *that,* and to be sensible about such decisions, we are going to have to refer to some central idea of function. A simple shopping list of aims or objectives will not do. If any program can be shown to serve *some* objective, then there is no way of deciding *among* programs. This is the source of the typical malady of the contemporary university, where policy is so visibly seen to arise from logrolling, mutual accommodations among established interests. This is why curriculum decisions so transparently turn on assuring that everyone gets a piece of the pie, why every discipline is a research priority, why it is so hard to terminate even the most mindless programs. There are simply no standards that can be appealed to, across fields, so that the fair-minded could decide what is crucial and outstanding, what is of lesser importance, and what is not good enough.

There is one requirement that any system of standards must meet. It must cut. It must actually *distinguish* good from bad performance, efficiency from error. Thus, we cannot, on the one hand, draw our lines of demarcation so broadly that they *include* all available cases or, on the other, draw them so tightly that they *exclude* all available cases.[8] The first failing normally comes from creating standards by empirical generalization. This is what universities in fact do, we say, and therefore, this is what they should do, and it is apparent that all meet the test. The second failing is that of utopian thinking, of comparing present practice with an imaginary, wished-for, alternative, say Socrates on one end of the log and the student on the other, and then lamenting the failure of *all* higher education to meet this ideal. Once again, we see the strong tension between theory and practice, the actual and the ideal, when we try to create tests that will distinguish the better from the worse in what is actually done.

If all our standards, all our aims, are of the same weight, on one level, then deliberation can come to no conclusion. Reason ends in simple assertion, a raw statement of preferences, or in infinite regression, always seeking a higher principle to arbitrate among contending lower-order ends.

We need an economizing principle, a maxim of choice, if we are to make reasonable decisions about the program of the university. This is also a requirement of justice. If we are going to *discriminate* among performances, say that some are more worthy, more important, than others, we are going to have to do so for good reason, on the basis of principle. For the essence of injustice is to discriminate, to treat cases differently, arbitrarily and whimsically, for no reason that is pertinent to the purpose at hand.

For those who think of economics as the endless calculation of gain, this idea that "economizing" has to do with judgments of excellence must seem wondrous indeed. However, I think this is the more essential sense of what economics is all about, as a fundamental activity of the mind. It is choice under pressure, where there are not resources, room enough or time, to do everything. And it is inherent in the quest for efficiency and excellence, to promote that which is best fitted to purpose and to weed out that which has failed to serve function well enough. Economizing, in this sense, is the practical element in morality. And, as we shall now see, it is closely linked to the political and the philosophical elements in practical reason.

The Political Element in Practical Reason

The reason we need economizing principles, criteria that distinguish better and worse alternatives, is that in the life of the university we are going to have to decide what is worth teaching and what is not. It is, in the end, the daunting responsibility of the university to *prescribe* a program for the life of the mind. In this sense, academic decisions are public and authoritative. They are *essentially* political. And it is the clearest counsel of our tradition of liberal democracy that public decisions must not be made arbitrarily. Those in authority must give good reasons for their choices, good reasons of public purpose. In any area of practical activity, this means that policies must be shown to be well suited to the aims of the venture at hand.

People pick up ideas in all sorts of ways. Some thoughts we create on our own. They are, as we say, the products of our imagination. Some ideas come easily, without effort. They simply "occur to us"—or they appear in dreams. Other things we "puzzle out," we "think through."

We get ideas, theories, visions, methods, from other people, helter-skelter, in no particular order, all the time: it is one of the commonest things we do. Some of these ideas we simply take to ourselves, spontaneously, naturally. We "understand" or we "pick up" a way of looking at things, a perspective. Other thoughts we are expected to know. We are taught them. We consciously learn. Some of the ideas of others, we know, are intended to manipulate us, with guile and cunning. Others, we understand, can benefit us if we can learn to take them as our own. They constitute technique, insight, therapy, revelation.

The peculiar, and fearful, task of the university is to scrutinize this sea of thought in which we live and to decide which among these musings, images, and speculations are worthy of affirmation and which are not, which are more useful, and which are foolishness and illusion.

This is, as I say, a political act, in the most essential meaning of that term. Of necessity, by virtue of its very nature, the university has the presumptuous responsibility for educating people to adopt certain habits of thought and to renounce others. What else can be its reason for being?

Once the full force of this sinks in, we recognize the paradox, unmistakably. The university is a pivotal institution of liberal democratic society. Yet liberalism, above all else, stands for freedom of thought and conscience, of the right of all opinions to be heard, of people to believe as they will. What then can justify the authority of the university to prescribe the acceptable habits of thought? Responding to the question takes us directly to the philosophical requirements of any theory of practical reason.

The Philosophical Element in Practical Reason

The judgment that the university must make about the worth of ideas depends directly on an estimate of what the mind can know. In a word, it requires an epistemology, a theory of knowledge. Our conception of the legitimacy both of the university's authority to prescribe a curriculum, and of the economizing principle we would endorse to decide among alternative approaches and teachings, depends, in the end, on the criteria we think it appropriate to invoke to distinguish truth from falsity, validity from illusion and error.

Within the contemporary university, as we shall see, the practical questions of epistemology are both curiously consensual and curiously contentious. The university, on the one hand, is unified, if by nothing else, by a general commitment to empiricist scientism (as long as one does not look too closely at what is meant by science, or empiricism). On the other hand, the university is riven by disputes and factions which have their roots, ostensibly, in large issues of how much the mind can know, whether there are reliable methods of reason, or whether reason itself is a fraud.

From Theory to Practice

So. In order to deliberate the program of the university from *within*, or appraise its performance from *without*, we are going to need a theory organized around a clear conception of the institution's central purpose. From this we can derive tests of the relative quality and importance of the university's specialized fields and programs which we can use when we must decide how to distribute emphasis among them. We will also develop an idea of how the university is properly governed. And these understandings will rest, as I suggested, on a conception of what it is possible for us to know.

Obviously, this way of talking about the economics, politics, and philosophy of higher education is a little different from what we have come to expect. Conventionally, we think of the economics of higher education as having to do with funding, budgeting, and such; the politics, with the university's responsiveness to various interests; and educational philosophy is usually associated with doctrines of pedagogy. Each of these subjects may be important in its own right, but here, I think, we are going a bit closer to the heart of the matter. I also think we shall find that the problems I shall raise are a lot more interesting.

It should also be apparent that these questions are not really the kind where the advice of the professional economist, political scientist, or philosopher is particularly helpful. The crucial considerations are interdependent, not specialized. Furthermore, the professional competence of scholars in these fields, particularly as they are constituted today, is not especially pertinent to the questions of practical reason.

At this point, I have said quite enough about practical reason in general. Further elaboration of the theme must be by example, as we go about developing a conception of what a university should do and how it should do it. It is time to set forth on the project itself, and the logical place to begin is by trying to understand prevailing practice.

CHAPTER TWO

The Rationale of the
Going Concern

Practical reason is an art of discovery. You do not begin by holding the world up to an ideal. Rather, you try to find one. In this, the method of practical reason shares philosophical pragmatism's general quarrel with Cartesianism, or any other form of a priori rationality. For to postulate, *in advance,* the form the solution *must* take would seem to foreclose the very possibility of learning something new. How could we then actually transform our thoughts about the nature of the world, or the rationale of our actions, through deliberate inquiry?

Thus we cannot begin by proposing an image of the aims of the university and simply use this to take stock of the institutions we know. Rather, we first have to try to understand what these universities, here before us, do and why they do things that way. Then, out of our doubts, queries, and criticisms, we gradually try to discern the pattern of an alternative.

In this scheme of reason, it is prevailing practice and not ideal archetype that is the basing point for judgment. Our aim is to reconsider unexamined custom and routine. But to do that sensibly, we first have to understand those customs and routines, and why some might think them wise and fully worthy of protection and preservation. And we do have to keep open the thought that the status quo *might* be the best option. In this respect, practical reason is quite unlike what is today often called, unhistorically, critical reason, where the object seems to be simply to show that all prevailing systems of thought, and all established institutions, have feet of clay. In practical reason, any alternative must be shown to be an improvement over prevailing practice. All of this may seem obvious enough, but it is an idea that runs strongly counter to many of the prevailing trends in the academy.

The American university subscribes to no official creed of educational purpose. It does not tell us, with any degree of candor or precision, how it plans to enhance human consciousness or transform our inner life. In fact, it is most reluctant to admit that it tries to do these things at all. It is remarkably silent, almost enigmatic, about its educational aims. But it has a history, and a peculiarly standardized pattern of structure and practice. From this, we should be able to infer what these institutions are intended to do.

What emerges is familiar enough. We instantly recognize the lineaments, the operating assumptions of the going concern and the rituals and routines that follow from them. The pattern becomes provocative and perplexing only when we ask whether the traits the university seems designed to insinuate and foster at every turn are in fact the traits which we think the liberally educated individual should possess.

I shall begin by discussing how the contemporary university seems to understand the life of the mind and how it portrays this life to students. I will go on to consider the rationale for its curiously fragmented, helter-skelter curriculum and how this could conceivably represent one meaning of the idea of "liberal" education. I conclude by arguing that although the university intimates that it is no more than a great heterodox bazaar, representing every conceivable approach to knowledge, it in fact communicates a very specific idea of the perspective, and the dispositions, of the educated person.

Education and the Marketplace of Ideas

Fundamentally, the American university thinks of itself as a knowledge factory. It was created to rationalize and systematize, in effect to industrialize, the pursuit of knowledge. This is part of our inheritance from the universities of Imperial Germany, particularly Berlin. This notion that scholarship is the organized production of knowledge represented an extraordinary reversal of all our historic ideals of learning, of the essential character of human thought.

In the most basic imagery of our civilization, it is the individual who is the thinker. Our stories of the genesis of ideas focus on the lone philosopher, the solitary genius, who sees freshly and for the very first time. The basic tenet of our liberal democratic political theory is that only the independent ideas of the free individual are trustworthy. The individual is, and ought to be, the source of thought and judgment. Liberalism goes to extraordinary lengths to try to create a setting in which individuals might be presumed free to "think for themselves."

But now the task of the university is to manufacture knowledge, and the work is understood to be a collaborative undertaking, not a solitary affair. The life of the mind is a common process. Great visions are rare and progress comes by small steps. Understanding emerges gradually through intricate, specialized organization and teamwork. Granted, one cannot plan discovery. This is not the place for hierarchic control. Scholars are not to be *assigned* problems by a master investigator. Rather, learning proceeds best as an open, self-organizing community, each member of which is motivated by a sense for evolving patterns of inquiry, a grasp of where the problems lie, where prospects of breakthrough beckon. This image of science as a self-organizing system is a powerful idea of purposeful solidarity. It is in fact how the university lives and it is part of what it teaches about the nature of thought. In the hands of political theorists as diverse as John Dewey and Friedrich Hayek, it becomes a metaphor for political order itself.[1] But this still comes as quite a surprise. This is not the idea of learning, or of community, that we actually expected the university to teach.

This collaborative image of scholarship influences our ideas of truth itself. Today, within the university, truth is generally understood not as individual illumination, insight or experience. Rather, the test of truth is intersubjectivity. A statement that is "worthy of belief" is one that has withstood painstaking scrutiny—repeated efforts to find it false, as Popperians would say.[2] It has been found significant and trustworthy from a variety of perspectives, in diverse applications. Thus, the fundamental guarantees of the worth of knowledge are collective, and this is generally taken as the criterion for establishing what the university is entitled to teach.

Thus, at one level, the university seems to understand its educational function as the simple transmission of knowledge. Its teaching task is to disseminate the fruits of research, those findings about the world that have been collectively corroborated and found useful. This conception of educational purpose, and only this, can explain such otherwise incomprehensible rituals as the large lecture method of instruction, the standardized textbook, and the objective examination.

Similarly, the idea of the university as rational producer of knowledge implies that inquiry is a progressive process. It unfolds over time. This part-Hegelian, part-Darwinian proposition, that mind emerges historically, that we are actually getting somewhere, is today seldom discussed openly, though it is often tacitly assumed, especially in the sciences. At the turn of the last century, however, when the American university was taking on its present form, this was a formidable philosophical proposition indeed, full of significance. For this implied that the routine everyday business of the university in seeking dependable and general statements was in fact to comprehend *logos,* the underlying order of things, which is to say, to discern, so far as finite and fallible minds were able, the intentions of God.[3]

This is one of the oldest ideas of the mission of the university. It is also, curiously enough, one of the most recent. To be sure, we no longer talk much about such things, but the startling fact is that there are radical, provocative notions behind the drab, familiar orthodoxy that we have come to expect from our institutions of higher learning. And the further we go, the more unsettling the implications of this idea of educational purpose will become.

The university came to think of itself as a shop. It made knowledge. This vision of mission altered the role model it taught. The scholar was no longer the person of broad talent and vision, the "man of letters." The ideal was now the master of discrete and limited technique, who played a specialized role in research, usually one too exotic for the layperson to comprehend. (To be sure, broad visions and big ideas were still important. After all, there has to be something to test. And in some disciplines one speaks, remarkably, of a division of labor between "theorists" and "experimentalists," as though these were simply different functions in the production process, as one would speak of machinists and painters in the factory.)

The very object of rationalization in any enterprise, the reason for system and standard technique, is to make outstanding talent and performance commonplace, to reduce the exceptional to routine. Thus one "deskills" scholarship and philosophy, much as craftsmanship is transformed into standard product, entrepreneurship into management, art into method, through systematic analysis of how virtuosity can be reduced to technique and rules of good practice. I say all this, by the way, without a note of irony.

In any event, as in many other once heroic callings, in science and scholarship quite ordinary mortals could now perform work previously thought reserved to those of rare talent. Once one understands this, a great deal about the life of the contemporary university begins to make sense, though one is still slightly surprised to find that the average academic department has no more people of genuine intellectual zest and broad enthusiasm than one is apt to find at a convention of stockmen, charter fishing boat operators, city managers, or restaurateurs.

All of this insinuates a particular conception of the life of the mind and of the aims of education and it is one that is at odds with longer traditions and ideals. The role model is the master of technique, not the reflective philosopher. The virtues to be cultivated are diligence, rigor, loyalty, and persistence, over boldness, rumination, and idle curiosity.

Education culminates, then, not in broad understanding but specialization: the major, graduate or professional training. The oft-repeated truism is that knowledge has grown too vast for any of us to master more than a bit of it. We should be modest in our aspirations. The aim is not to seek after truth or wisdom, but to receive an analytic power as a trust from the hard-won common stock of demonstrated, reliable skill, to put it to use in some worthwhile endeavor, as a participant in a complex process in which one is prepared to play a limited but crucial role.

Thus expressed, this is not an altogether unattractive ideal. There is a certain humility in regarding the intellectual as research worker rather than sage, as a craftsman rather than a genius. There is a sense of solidarity, and egalitarianism, in regarding good practice in any vocation as worthy, so that a—literally—masterful performance in chemistry or philosophy is very much the same as one in aviation or cooking.

As I said earlier, the educational ideal of the American research university is familiar enough. Yet it is, in a way, still startling and strangely disconcerting. Thus we can begin our deliberations. Precisely what is it here that we find unsettling, what is it that does not quite square with our ideas of what liberal education is supposed to accomplish?

The Structure of the Disciplines

In the first decades of the twentieth century, the American university was comprehensively rationalized. The rationalization of the university meant that any subject that was worth teaching had to be constituted as a discipline, with the full paraphernalia of journals, associations, graduate programs, and the like. It also meant that a discipline had to possess distinctive methods and a body of certified knowledge created by those methods. The search for the apparatus of professional legitimacy was on, and it led to wrenching controversies in many areas of study. Many of these disputes are still going on. They frame some of the most basic philosophic controversies of our century: whether social science is possible, for example, of whether science can be read as a literary text.

The sciences provided the core model of how a learned discipline should be constituted. The crucial question was whether other disciplines, the social studies and the humanities, could be structured like science. Gerald Graff traces the history of the notion that the teacher of literature had to be a professional critic, and that to be a critic meant to employ an identifiable technique of criticism. In part, the point was to show that the teaching of English required specialized skill. Literature was considered a "soft" subject in comparison with classics. The object was to make it *harder.* Graff quotes H. C. G. Brandt, a protagonist of professional criticism:

A scientific basis dignifies our profession. . . . by introducing scientific methods, we shall show before very long that everybody cannot [teach English], that the teacher has to be specially and as scientifically trained for his work in our department as in any other.[4]

The idea that *philosophy,* the whole activity of self-conscious thought, should be structured as a profession, reduced to the form of any other department, is one of the more disquieting outcomes of this transformation of the idea of the university. Daniel J. Wilson describes the development of philosophy as a specialized discipline in America. In the formative years of the research university, in the age of William James, philosophy and psychology were generally assumed to be interwoven aspects of the study of mind. Soon, however, psychology broke off to pursue its inquiries according to militantly experimental methods. Philosophy, in its turn, went off in seemingly unending quest of some idea of what *professional* philosophy could conceivably mean.[5]

But it is in the social studies that the search for appropriate method and scientific standing has had the most profound consequences for the educational program of the university. The array of social science disciplines—sociology with its holistic view that human nature is best studied in aggregates and groups, economics with its paradigm of rational choice, anthropology with its culture concept and preoccupation with man-as-species, psychology intent on discovering causes of human behavior that run deeper than reasons—represents little more than a conspectus of fundamental cleavages between contending schools of thought as they existed at the end of the last century, now frozen into place, preserved beyond fundamental reconsideration, in the curriculum of the university. It might seem that psyche, society, culture, state, and economy add up to a logical set, but one could imagine other ways of doing it. If politics, why not family? If psyche and society, why not inquiry itself? While we have come to accept this array as logical, the historic fact is that it is a matter of accident. It could have been otherwise. Nonetheless, the important point is that the outsider, the student, does not quite realize what is going on, that what one learns from a general education in these disciplines is not the proper study of humankind in itself, but the terms of an almost forgotten controversy about that study. There is nothing inevitable about the arrangement. It is, for many purposes, merely of historical interest. One goes to economics not to learn about "the economy" but to receive instruction in a particular mode of thought about human interaction. The relationship of the method to the actual workings of the productive institutions of society is tenuous at best.

To be sure, not all the social studies are based on research traditions that could be institutionalized within the new universities. Political science, for example, was created because it was thought not so much that there *was* a science of politics as that there ought to be one, that democratic government, like manufacture, agriculture, or home economics, would benefit from systematic, thoughtful analysis. But note that this is a rare case in which educational purpose dictated the formation of a discipline. The more usual approach was to institutionalize an existing school of thought.

This methodical, uniform, process of the creation of disciplines, each the repository of authority to prescribe a program of research and instruction, and to determine the qualifications of faculty in the field, leads to a very specific idea of the university itself. The university is to be understood, fundamentally, as an administrative arrangement, a holding company for the set of organized disciplines. It is, itself, empty of philosophy. It has nothing to say, really, about what will and will not be taught. That authority is vested in the departments. Granted, universities may claim a petty distinctiveness by the way they distribute emphasis among the disciplines, or by cultivating quirks of tradition or ambience. Granted, the university may use its budget to allocate resources, and thus establish priorities among the recognized fields of study at the margin. But these decisions are normally understood as questions of economics, certainly not of educational philosophy.

Basically, the curricular task of the university is the assembly of fabricated parts, of finished components. It does not consider the big picture. *Nobody* considers the big picture. Education arises from the loose coordination of the discrete programs of the learned professions. And there is no prevailing sense of necessary relation or priority among the fields. All recognized disciplines have equal standing. Folklore is the same as philosophy, mathematics no more or no less important than the exotic languages.

Granted, there is a constant evolutionary process going on. Entrepreneurs champion new disciplines, schisms occur, hybrids develop. To some extent, the university shepherds this process of innovation, consolidation, and correction. However, it is remarkable how little the growth of the sheer number of programs and disciplines in this century has affected the basic structure of knowledge that was institutionalized at the founding. The core disciplines have changed but little. Most growth has been in the applied fields, and here, pecuniary or political interest more often explains the evolutionary process than intellectual advance. When such applied or practical disciplines appear, they must be invested with the full trappings of professional reputability—the peer-reviewed journals, the national conventions with portentious panels and papers—but it is never quite clear to what extent this results in the development of credible and rigorous analysis in a field created to satisfy some political or monied interest and how much of this is essentially fraud. No general rule can be given. In some of these disciplines-in-response-to-interest, research and instruction are a mockery of the work of the intellect. But in other of the so-disdained departments, the quality of research and instruction is often far more rigorous, alive, and telling than in the prestigious basic fields which may be, by now, simply going through the motions.

Liberal Education and the Marketplace of Ideas

Now the specialized, fragmented teachings of the contemporary research university may seem the very antithesis of what we normally mean by liberal education. But in its original conception, the newly transformed university was supposed to represent an educational program uniquely compatible with the political ideals of liberalism. Let me explain.

Our inheritance from the German university includes not only the notion that the university's main mission is the systematic production of knowledge but a very specific principle of academic freedom as well. The ideal has two complementary parts. On one side is the absolute right of professors to teach as they see fit. This is *Lehrfreiheit*. It implies protection not simply against political control but, more significantly, against one's colleagues. Thus, while the scholarly professions are the guarantors of the worth of knowledge, the arbiters of what should be taught by the university, the strongest right of tenured professors is that of defying their professions. This means that, in the end, there is little collective responsibility for the program of the university. Though in theory, the profession is the trustee of content and competence, there is a strong presumption that professors have virtually absolute authority in their own classrooms.

Lernfreiheit was the opposite side of this ideal of academic freedom. It meant that students had a right to study what and as they thought best. In America, this implied the replacement of the prescriptive curriculum by the free elective system.

The uniform curriculum of the nineteenth-century colleges began with Latin and Greek, both to instill rigor and as a means of teaching logic, grammar, and rhetoric; passed through mathematics, natural philosophy, geology, biology, and astronomy, which led to studies in philosophy; and culminated in a course in moral philosophy, normally taught by the college president.[6]

Then all of this was swept away. Charles Eliot of Harvard abolished the prescriptive curriculum and instituted the free elective system. Now there was to be no necessary relationship among courses and no implied hierarchy or progression. As Eliot said,

> This university recognizes no real antagonism between literature and science, and consents to no such narrow alternatives as mathematics or classics, science or metaphysics. We should have them all, and at their best. To observe keenly, to reason soundly, to imagine vividly are operations as essential as that of clear and forcible expression, and to develop one of these faculties, it is not necessary to repress and dwarf the others.[7]

To be sure, Eliot's scheme was too radical even for Harvard, and his successor, Lawrence Lowell, instituted a system of distribution requirements. Thus was born the familiar pattern of general education, understood as "breadth," leading to specialization, or "depth," represented by the major, which has become, with only modest variations and tinkerings here and there, the standard format of American higher education.

The free elective system suggests a specific idea of liberal education, and it is one strikingly compatible with certain bedrock public ideals of our civilization.

The fundamental first premise of political liberalism is that the state should not be the arbiter of human purposes. It is up to individuals to assess life's prospects, to determine what is worth doing and what is not, what to affirm and what to deny, with whom to associate and for what ends. The state should not be the architect of social order. That should emerge spontaneously, from the free choice of individuals to coordinate their efforts, to join in solidarity to promote certain ends.

Ideally then, all associations of the liberal society are to be understood as forms of contract. The transactions of buyers and sellers determine the pattern of the economy, and similar patterns of contract among potential engagements legitimate the bonds of religion, learning, community, the family itself. Even the state is supposed to be rightful only if it can be shown to be founded on a social contract that a reasonable individual might accept.

It is in this spirit that the free elective system can be seen as a program of liberal education. The university was to be understood as a marketplace of ideas. As in other marketlike arrangements, pattern and order emerge out of uncoerced individual choice. No authoritative decisions are made about what ought to be taught, about what an educated person should know. Rather, faculty decide what is of value to teach (subject to minimal and normally congenial collegial oversight) and students decide what they think it is important to learn. The choices of each are constrained by those of the other. Faculty can teach only that for which there is a demand, students can learn only that which faculty feel they are warranted in teaching.

Such a conception of the university would seem to square both with the liberal principle of individual choice and the ideal of freedom of thought and expression. However, there is an important difference between academic and political freedom. Academic freedom has never connoted the right to say anything one pleases in the classroom. We do not believe that the university is just another forum of public debate. The scholar's right is, for us, not that of simple freedom of speech but the right personally to interpret a recognized subject according to the rules of good practice of a discipline. And this means that the metaphor of the market does not automatically resolve the problems of the right and responsibility of the academy to prescribe the better habits of mind, the greater texts, and the more significant corpus of knowledge.

We encounter other difficulties when we take the market as the model for the university. In economic theory, authentic market choice requires complete information, but it is simply inherent in the nature of the "product" of the university that students cannot appraise the value of what they choose to learn until after they have been taught. In this, at least, choice among academic programs is quite unlike choice among refrigerators or brands of canned tuna.

Further, I am not sure that we want to say that the object of education is to secure the highest degree of "consumer satisfaction" according to the hedonistic principles of conventional market economics. Granted, today liberal education often seems to mean little more than a random selection of courses, chosen "just as one pleases," from the great cafeteria of knowledge. (In my university, more than four thousand courses can be used to fulfill the basic distribution requirements for the baccalaureate degree.) Semester after semester, students may calculate an optimum mix of the momentarily intriguing, convenient, and relatively undemanding, with little overall point or purpose. Surely, this is not what we have in mind. The liberal idea of academic freedom we inherited implied that students *would prescribe for themselves* a curriculum that was best suited to their intellectual purposes. But the simple idea of the university as market does not seem sufficient for us to make good on this responsibility.

The fact of the matter is that the market model does not really resolve the question of the political character of the university, of the right of the faculty to determine what shall be taught and what shall be excluded from the domain of authorized teachings. We cannot say that faculty are free to teach purely as they wish and that, in the end, the curriculum takes form as a response to demand. It just doesn't work that way. Nor, in the end, do I think we will want it to.

There are several well-known defenses of the free-form, laissez-faire program of the university. In the end they only reopen the question of whether this is, indeed, what we expect the university to accomplish.

Perhaps the most widespread view is that the study of a broad variety of subjects teaches students to think. The subject matter is incidental: the aim is to inculcate a certain habit of mind. Thus, the point is to learn not botany but the scientific attitude, not political theory but abstract reasoning, not sociology but a certain skepticism about the professed rationale of dominant institutions. There is quite a lot to be said for this view, of course. The difficulty is that *any* discipline can claim to provide good intellectual exercise. For years, we recall, it was said that Greek and Latin should be studied to discipline the mind. The problem with this approach is that it yields no economizing principle, and no criteria for the critique of performance. It is simply an irrebuttable case for the status quo.

The other obvious defense of the free market university is that it is efficiently designed for the task of producing academic specialists. The function of the liberal education courses, the "breadth" requirements, is simply to *introduce* students to the diverse professional disciplines. Most instructors unquestioningly assume that the function of the basic courses, the "core" liberal arts curriculum, is to "interest" students in their subject and provide instruction necessary for more advanced work; in other words, to recruit and prepare potential majors. (My own discipline is unusual in that the basic course is normally an introduction to American government rather than an introduction to political science.)

Are we to understand then that the aim of liberal education is to provide a kind of "exhibit" of the works of the university? Is it our intent that the liberally educated person is one who is well acquainted with the academic division of labor? Is it as though understanding the life of the university is equivalent to understanding the life of the world?

The Education of the Detached Observer

But there might be something that holds this fragmented system of education together. The university claims that it is open and pluralistic, impartial among the many contending approaches to knowledge. It is also possible to argue, however, that a strong integrating theme runs through the curriculum, that the university intimates in all its works and all its ways that there is an appropriate way to approach all problems of the mind. This is from the position of the detached observer.

The attitude of clinical "objectivity" is reinforced throughout the curriculum. In the natural sciences, it is taken for granted that the aim is to explain an external order of nature. In literature, the text is an object to be interpreted. In politics, government is a phenomenon to be analyzed. Everywhere, it is intimated that the stance of the educated person should be that of the spectator.[8]

The point of view of the official empiricism of the learned professions is that of the outsider looking in. But practical reason requires an "insider's" perspective. The participant is not spectator but protagonist. The point of analysis is not simply to find causes for a pattern of action but to grasp its rationale, to see what commends it as a way of doing things. Practical reason necessarily means to advocate one plan against alternatives. There is nothing "value neutral" about it. Criticism is not simply interpretation but the effort to rethink assumptions, to consider improvements in style and method. And note, in practical reason one is neither objective nor detached but *committed* to the endeavor in question.

To teach science as participating in the enterprise of physics or geology is much different from (and richer than) teaching it simply as observation and explanation. To teach literature from the point of view of the writer is much different from teaching it from that of the critic. To teach politics as a matter not so much of what *they* are doing to you as of what *you* might very well be doing to *them,* as citizen, as representative, as adjudicator, requires different skills, and a different frame of mind.

Now, of course, there is no incompatibility between the two modes of reason. The very detachment which characterizes scientific empiricism is essential to the exercise of practical reason. We have to stand back, to see our present convictions as something "out there" to be consciously analyzed, if we are to become self-consciously reflective about matters of purpose and method. (It is also true, though, that to *lose* oneself in a project may be the condition of great art, great science, or great statecraft, that to see one's endeavor in perspective might be to lose the fine edge of creativity or daring.)

It is true that in the applied fields, scientific and practical reason tend to be taught together. In medicine, engineering, agriculture, one learns to adopt both the stance of the scientist and that of the practitioner, to let the habits of cautious, dispassionate observation and deliberate action enhance one another. It is rather in the basic disciplines, in the core liberal arts curriculum, that I fear that the university, despite protestations of the most open intellectual pluralism, in fact teaches a singular, rather limited, conception of the appropriate methods and objects of thought.

Scientific empiricism does rather drastically narrow the range of legitimate intellectual concerns. In the contemporary university, one quickly learns that certain questions are out of order. One does not ask persistently about what ought to be done, for normative questions entail what are called value judgments, and these are said to be beyond the scope of scientific analysis. Furthermore, one should not ask big questions about the point of it all. Issues of what it all means are particularly awkward. We no longer admit (though this was the very purpose of classical science) *teleological* questions—questions about great designs or designers—into our inquiries. The only pertinent question seems to be to see if one can discern regularity and pattern in a universe that is taken to be one of brute, material, random activity.

Now all of this does tend to dampen interest in some of the most important things that people care about. And it does tend to inhibit the exercise of precisely those analytical faculties which are essential to practical reason. For practical reason is concerned specifically with how things ought to be done, with good and bad performance, correctness and error, and all of this in relation to some clear conception of point and purpose.

To some extent, the problem comes about because philosophic pragmatism, which was the regnant spirit in which the new American universities were formed, was gradually replaced by a positivist conception of science as the twentieth century moved along.[9] In philosophical pragmatism, there is no sharp separation of scientific and practical reason, action and inquiry.[10] Mind and matter, subject and object, are intimately related in the process of thought. In philosophic pragmatism, action is the aim of detached analysis, and the worth of scientific statements is established by what they mean in human action, and how they pertain to human purposes. In positivist conceptions of science, however, there is strict insistence on the detached observer perspective, on value neutrality, and the sharp separation of the knowing subject and the object of inquiry.

The sharp separation of subject and object, the idea that we should see the world from the outside-looking-in, has implications at a number of levels. At the deepest, it affects our entire view of human consciousness.

The tacit assumption of much contemporary education is that most of what goes on in the subject, the mind, is untrustworthy. The internal life is full of illusion, fantasy, passion, partiality, and self-interest. We can trust the vagaries of thought only when they check out against the hard facts of raw matter. The purpose of education is to chastise and discipline the mind, to make it aware of its own propensity to illusion, to fix it on the contemplation only of what is *really* there. In such a conception of the aims of education—which I think is no caricature—one senses a strange mingling of themes reminiscent of Calvinism, Enlightenment empiricism, Nietzschean irrationalism, and Freudian psychology.

Many, I think, would affirm precisely this vision of the role of the university. Some would take it as the essence of scientific understanding. In the process, however, we should not ignore or suppress the fact that the classic conception of science worked precisely the other way around. The project of rational understanding that began in Greece, was exemplified by Plato and Aristotle as well as the pre-Socratics, and more than we are generally willing to admit today inspired *our* science, from Copernicus and Newton to Einstein, Heisenberg, and beyond, presumed precisely that the "hard facts" of the material world were transient and illusory, they *could* be otherwise, and that the aim was to discern that which was permanent and unchanging beneath the appearances of a universe of change and flux. What we were after were the principles of order and development, the underlying reason of the world.

Now to teach such a perspective today, seriously, not just as another "topic," another "text" in a survey of ideas, would be decidedly suspect, perhaps "unprofessional." As I say, we no longer deal seriously in arguments from design or underlying purpose. Only explanations cast as observed regularities in meaningless matter will do.

The distrust of subjectivity has some remarkable implications for the whole process of liberal education. In the social sciences, to follow the ancient imperative and seek to "know thyself" can only mean to come to understand oneself as an object. The "self" is a construct of categories. One *is* extrovert, ethnic, homo sapiens, liberal, what have you. One *validates* one's life by looking at it as a fact, out there, pinpointing it in the web of externalized, objective relationships among beings and objects.

At the more sophisticated levels, to be sure, we know better than this. It is perfectly well understood that subject and object, mind and the world, are interdependent, woven together. Scientific understanding is a matter of deep subjectivity. Scientific theory is not a simple *reflection* of the world but a deliberately contrived picture of how the world might be. And there is no such thing as the pure detached observer. All of our observations of the "brute facts" are shaped and shaded by theoretical presuppositions and expectations. You see a fern as a sporophyte because that's how our system of botanical classification works. God knows what a fern *really* is.

To be sure, scientific thinking is not just imagining, spinning webs, as you please, about the world out there. The facts resist. They do fight back. So knowledge is, today, philosophically often understood as a give and take between mind and the world. But this means we have to trust subjectivity, in all its possibilities, just as much as, perhaps a bit more than, the world of hard facts, out there.

The implications of all of this are staggering—and controversial. On the one hand are those who stress the point that those reflections on the world that we call science are made up. They are contingent. They could be otherwise. At the extreme, the case is made that science is just another story, no better or worse in terms of truth than myth or poetry.[11] At the other end are those who take the most important purpose of mind to be to grasp the world. They follow in the tradition of Plato and Aristotle, more recently perhaps that of Hegel, Peirce, or Teilhard de Chardin.

Now you can learn all of this in the contemporary American university. You can learn this, for example, if you study the history and philosophy of science rather than the core sciences themselves. Generally, however, such discussion is reserved only for the very advanced courses: it is a mystery to be revealed only to the initiates, the adepts. Or it is presented in a vague tone of subversion, as though to unmask the pretense and futility of the established order. Either way is an odd manner in which to learn about thought, about the relationship of mind to the world. And, of course, in most of the basic courses that are supposed to provide a *liberal* education, the subject never comes up at all.

But even were we to teach all the nuances of the contemporary understanding of scientific inquiry, we would still not have re-solved the problem with which we began. For it is still taken for granted that the primary task of mind is to understand the world. We still have to settle the question of whether we think the proper work of the university is the cultivation of those singular qualities of mind appropriate to the systematic observer, to the possible neglect of other qualities of thought, other objects of curiosity, other works of sensitivity, the cultivation of other forms of care and responsibility, of craft, nurture, and stewardship.

There will be opportunity enough to consider all of this as we move along. At this juncture, I would focus simply on one point concerning prevailing practice. Can the contemporary university have it both ways? Can it represent itself as an open marketplace of ideas and yet teach a *particular* doctrine of the proper work of reason? Now the problem of our inquiry becomes clear. If we can-not sustain present practice in face of this dilemma, which direc-tion shall we move to resolve it? Shall we say that we must pre-sume *less* authority to prescribe the life of the mind, that we must open the academy to a wild divergence of opportunities for ex-pression and thought? Or shall we say that we might very well presume to prescribe *more,* that there are methods of analysis as reputable as those we presently teach which we neglect to our peril or shame? Thus do we open Pandora's box, but warily and gin-gerly, fully conscious of all the ancient enigmas and current quar-rels that will be loosed, and with which we will have to reckon.

CHAPTER THREE

Purpose: What Do We Expect a University to Do?

Let us reflect. What do we expect a university to do? An institution that deals in the power of the mind can perform many useful social roles. It can be defender of the faith. It can underwrite the ideology of the regime. It can train specialists to sustain a capitalist economy. Certainly a case can be made that the university should perform each of these functions, and just as certainly a case can be made that it should perform none of them. We seem to be entering upon a fundamental controversy.

However, appearances can be deceiving. There may be more common ground here than meets the eye. Perhaps there should be a political, a religious, or an economic *dimension* to the university's teaching. But I do not think we would be willing to define any one of these objectives as the essential point of the venture. I think we have a common sense that a university which became primarily an instrument of political or religious indoctrination, or merely a source of skilled workers, would be corrupt. It would not be a university, in fact.

Now I know perfectly well that there are those who profess that the meanings we attach to institutions are merely conventional. In *Alice in Wonderland* fashion, they feel we are free to call a university a church, or a family a friendship, "just as we please." But this is merely playing with words. The more fundamental point is that whether we call it family or not, we are going to have to have some arrangements for the care and nurture of the young. Whether we call them "courts" or not, we must have some means of adjudicating disputes. And whether we think of them as "universities" or not, we will have to have some shared methods of deliberative inquiry. We are talking about basic human propensities and purposes, what Aristotle called "natural associations."

Of course, we can organize these practices in all sorts of ways, invest them with all kinds of meaning. The standard case of the skeptic is that there is no basis for judging among these practices. They are just different ways of doing things. But do we not, *as a matter of fact* (and across humanity), reflect on and appraise these diverse practices? Do we not sometimes conclude that some give expression to some human potentiality that others do not? Do we not, despite our ethnocentrism, at times conclude that the ways of other people might actually be preferable to our own?

So we are going to have to begin by renouncing pure skepticism if we are going to engage in practical reason or, for that matter, if we are even going to account for our *capacity* to engage in practical reason. If practical reason is possible at all, we are going to have to assume that we can refer to an idea of essential purpose, of the meaning and point of a human activity, even though our grasp of that idea be vague and halting, even if, in our ignorance, we argue mightily over its meaning and its implications.

How do we explain our capacity for *corrigibility?* Our ability to discern excellence and error, to talk of better and worse performance, to *correct* our actions, to improve them, is among the more elemental mysteries. It is all very well and good to say that our norms and values, our ideas of purpose and the ends of institutions, are given by tradition. But this does not account for the fact that we persistently appraise this inheritance, that somehow we are able to say that not only our customs but even our *values* might not be as good as they could be.

How on earth do we do this? It is possible to say that our idea of the university, or of any of our institutions and practices, is a specific cultural inheritance, a peculiar artifact of history. Other peoples might construct an entirely different image of the enterprise, and we too, in the fullness of time, may come to think differently about it. And it is wise to acknowledge this much, for there is no reason to assume that we *already* know the ideal requirements of any human activity. But none of this explains how our capacity for appraisal and self-correction is possible at all. We might as well simply postulate a human capacity to seek and discern purpose, to derive notions of right action from such ideas, and to identify such inquiries ultimately with some fundamental human power, need, or yearning. And with that, of course, we end up right back in the arms of Aristotle.

So if we dare to say that some ideas of the university are *mistaken,* that it does not seem right to define the university's purpose as indoctrination according to the ideologies of a regime or a cult, we have said very much indeed. For the implication of such convictions is that we do not regard the question of the university's function as simply up for grabs. We imply that the argument can have a rational structure. The purpose of the university is not simply a matter of opinion, a question that can be settled by counting noses or balancing interests. And that declaration is the price of admission to the exercise of practical reason.

We do not have to settle the matter all at once, declare for some majestic proposition that would lay all contention about the aims of the university to rest. We can simply go on from here, and see how far we can get in finding what we dimly suspect is common ground. So the first step, apparently, is to find out what we already seem to know.

The Public and the Intrinsic Purposes of the University

Let me propose a basic distinction. Let me say that education is the public purpose of the university and inquiry its intrinsic function. When we think about the aims of education, we are asking how we want to go about nurturing and enhancing the powers of mind, what knowledge, beliefs, and values we want cultivated, generally and systematically, among the people. When we ask about the aims of inquiry, we are concerned with how we will go about finding out and learning how to know.

My case will be that there is a fundamental tension between

these objectives, and that in exploring this tension and trying to resolve it we may come closer to grasping our underlying conception of purpose, our reasoned idea of what a university should do. I think we will find that pursuing either one of these objectives at the expense of the other leads to identifiable error. So our course must lie somewhere between the two extremes.

Let us start on one horn of the dilemma and proceed to the other. If education is a public function, why is it not a fundamental right of a free and democratic people to try to shape its common temper and quality of mind? The university will inevitably encourage some habits of thought and spirit and discourage others. Why then should we not consider the definition of the aims of liberal education and, hence, the purpose of the university to be ideally a self-conscious *political* act?[1]

But we would not think that a university that taught precisely as it was told, even by the sovereign people, was a university at all. It would be at best a school, at worst a propaganda agency. A university does not teach mindlessly. It is supposed to *scrutinize* its teachings, to criticize, reexamine, and reformulate received ideas. A university is supposed to "think for itself." This is essential to our idea of the university. This is what we expect a university to do.

But does this mean that we actually think that the university "knows better," that it has capacity to distinguish truth from falsity, right from wrong, rationality from error? Are we willing to let not only these questions but the overall tone and character of our civilization be decided by the "experts"? Great themes of political theory are obviously in contention here. But unlike the great schools of political thought, we are actually going to have to decide the question, in the practical realm of affairs. And unlike many protagonists in the public debate, I for one do not think that the answer is altogether obvious. I do not think we expect the university to teach just as the citizens want or just as the academics deem fit.

Again, my thought is that in probing and pondering this tension, we may come closer to an understanding of what we are trying to achieve through the workings of this strangely familiar yet strangely complex and mysterious institution. Let us start then by considering certain conventional views of the aims of liberal education, and ask whether the university could, with integrity, commit itself to one of them as the centerpiece and rationale of its educational mission.

The Public Purpose of the University

Enculturation

Let us begin at what seems the natural beginning and propose that the task of education is to initiate the young into the way of life of a people. The professoriate then are like the elders of the tribe. Such a notion of the essential purpose of education rests on sound philosophic ground. We are political animals. We come to the fullness of our powers never alone but only as members of an organized, self-conscious community, one which has figured out an idea of the world and of our place in it. We *are* what our culture enables and permits us to be, and we *exist* as persons of a particular place and point in history. In our philosophical heritage, the point is most notably associated with Aristotle and Hegel, though any historically oriented philosopher might do as well.

On this understanding, education is above all useful. The object is to learn how to do things *our* way, so that one can get along, can cope, and also become a constructive, contributing member of the community. One begins by learning the more crucial skills: our language, our ways of calculating, our manners and morals, our rituals and beliefs. One goes on to the more intimate mysteries: what we imagine the universe and God to be, what we think the creative force is at its most beautiful.

A liberal education is then broad based. The aim is to be in touch with the manifold understandings of the society, its universe of shared meanings. It is, for those who see its essence as "cultural literacy," to know what happened in the Lincoln-Douglas debates, how lasers work, how Marx and Darwin are related, and what befell at the Congress of Vienna.[2]

For many, one subtle advantage of this approach is that it seems to sidestep thorny epistemological thickets. One does not teach that scientific procedure is the unique route to reliable knowledge, or that legitimate governments rest on the consent of the governed, or that noncontradiction is a condition of rational assertion. One teaches rather that scientific method, liberal democratic politics, and rationality are in effect "the customs of our people." The university proclaims no absolutes. It makes no judgments. It is simply passing on a heritage.[3]

Further, if one teaches the heritage historically, as is conventional, the point is to show how we came to think about things as we do. There is thus no necessity to our habits of thought. We did things differently in the past. We could do them differently again in the future. Everything is contingent. In such ways, this conception of the purpose of liberal education is made consistent with the spirit of rational skepticism and relativism which is so much a generally held value in the culture of the contemporary university.

And the problem, of course, is that this position cannot be sustained. The university does not just "pass on" a tradition. It creates a story that gives the tradition point and meaning. It draws a moral from it. It is up to the university to *find* meaning in the tradition. That is part of its intrinsic function. But as it does this, it has to make manifest its theory of interpretation, its economizing principle, if its teaching is to be public and legitimate. For the university cannot teach *everything*. It must select, it must define the tradition. And, as we all know, that principle of selection is today at the heart of stormy academic controversy.

Today there is a strong faction in the university that argues, in effect, that the actual, if unacknowledged, purpose of teaching the tradition is to extol the virtues, beliefs, and habits of mind of the white, male-dominated cultures of Western Europe and North America. This is what enculturation comes down to in the end. The specific tradition of this culture is taught as though its traits and modes of thinking were superior and universal. Thus is the university implicated in the systematic domination of a system that underwrites exploitative capitalism, political hegemony, and the environmental destruction of the earth. The accusation is *precisely* that to accept enculturation as defining educational purpose is to pursue a notion of the public function of the university that fundamentally corrupts its intrinsic mission. It cannot claim objectivity or detachment for such teachings. It cannot claim that its teachings result from the critical scrutiny of the plausible alternatives. The very definition of the mission *excludes* vast reaches of human experience. The remedy is to profess a less partisan conception of culture.

Those who advocate multicultural education today in fact have many different objectives in mind. Some merely want to represent diverse perspectives and heritages within the curriculum, to encourage simple tolerance and understanding, to nurture pride and self-respect among minorities. Some basically want to broaden our conception of what counts as "contribution," others to remove encrusted and unexamined prejudices from the curriculum. (And it would be odd if courses in The Contemporary Novel, let us say, systematically excluded writings by women, or by authors from outside North America or Europe.) But at the more problematic level, the case against teaching the tradition is that there is no particularly good reason to give special respect, and priority treatment, to the legacies of philosophic and political discourse, the heritage of scientific understanding, the masterpieces of literature, art, and thought that are represented as the specific and treasured inheritance of the West.

Thus is the idea of "teaching the tradition" hoist on its own petard. For if *all* we are teaching is a tradition, then one way of life is as valid in its own terms as another, and then it is far more responsible to teach students that there *are* multiple viewpoints, diverse ways of knowing, than to insist on the priority, if not the superiority, of the ways of the West.

Now, of course, there are many in the contemporary university who are oblivious to all of this. They simply presume that they are teaching science, or economics, or philosophy, or art. They do not regard their standards of scientific statement, or rational inference, or style, as a cultural artifact. Rather they believe that there *are* standards of reason, independent of context, universal in application, by which *all,* independent of cultural legacy, may judge the credibility of statements, the trustworthiness of observations and beliefs, the excellence or utility of a human performance. The fact that such standards arose in what is loosely called "the West" is simply curious and accidental. On this account, teaching the tradition is not the centerpiece but the handmaiden of the real work of the university. And in that case, there is no need for what is taught, in any field, to be balanced so as to represent diverse ethnic, cultural, and gender points of view. One teaches best practice. What matters in deciding whether to include or exclude any given text is the significance of the argument, not the characteristics of its author.

Should enculturation define the university's essential purpose? The tension between the intrinsic and the public function of the institution is now quite obvious. If we discount the possibility that the university can invoke standards independent of culture, then we must declare that the university can only teach the tradition, and the question of how it should define and construe the tradition is *strictly* a political question, one that will be settled by the assertion of power and control. And that is how many within the university, and perhaps many in the public at large, in fact understand the matter.

But if we take the intrinsic function seriously, if we assert that the university plays an autonomous role in the appraisal of thought, then enculturation, pure and simple, can never be a workable or worthy objective. We acknowledge then that the university must, of necessity, *interpret* a culture, decide what to emphasize and what to ignore. To do this legitimately it must invoke standards that are, in some sense, independent of culture itself. But in that case it is far more important to teach these standards than the inherited meanings and artifacts of a civilization, no matter how treasured. The object now is that students learn how to distinguish the better performance, the more trustworthy theory, the more meaningful construction of ideas.

The Education of Citizens

Perhaps enculturation is too imprecise an aim. In our heritage, it is often simply taken for granted that the proper purpose of education is the development of citizens. The theme is persistent in American educational philosophy, from Jefferson and Mann to Dewey and Meiklejohn.[4] In this case, liberal education would literally become "the education of liberals."

But is it at all clear what the education of citizens requires? Liberal democracy is not a tight, well-ordered doctrine, but a rather loose collection of contentious ideas. Now that we no longer debate the great "isms," most of the arguments of political philosophy are *within* liberal democratic theory and *about* the adequacy of various formulations of this ideal as a public philosophy. Thus, instead of arguing liberal democracy *against* Marxism, fascism, and the like, we now argue the rival merits of free market, natural rights, utilitarian, and pragmatic liberalism, participatory, communitarian, or representative democracy, and civic republicanism. Each version of liberal democratic theory has different imperatives, and each suggests a very different program for the education of citizens.

To some it seems of first importance and no more than truism that liberal education should teach people to "think for themselves." The proper "education of liberals" is the systematic cultivation of skepticism. Liberal democracy presumes individual freedom, personal choice, and moral autonomy. The great danger to liberal democracy comes from the "impairments" to free thought: unexamined beliefs, imposed by tradition, convention, consensus, or indoctrination.[5] Thus, it is the primary business of the university to teach mistrust for inherited or conventional beliefs, to show the "irrationality" of—or the political interests that benefit from—established patterns of thought.

Is this really what we have in mind? Is it really our intent that students should come to mistrust the entire body of established thought, that they should think no idea worthwhile unless they have come to it entirely on their own? It often seems that way, when one examines the everyday practices of higher education and the formal rationale given for them. But how do we square this "individualizing" and "liberating" conception of education through the systematic inculcation of doubt (is this all a throwback to Descartes?) with the parallel motif of the contemporary university, that knowledge is the product of systematic, cumulative, collaborative effort?

(Of course, skepticism is essential to scientific rationalism but there the purpose is different. The aim is continuing scrutiny of a body of thought to the end that it be refined and perfected. The point of doubt is not to free the individual but to enhance the common project.)

But there is a certain sense in which educating individuals to think for themselves is essential to the integrity of the liberal democratic regime. If liberalism is to make sense as a form of political economic organization, one has to assume that individuals

are competent choosers. The legitimacy of any contractual relationship—and all relationships in a liberal society are suppoed to
be contractual—depends on equality among the parties, and this
requires that each individual understand fully the personal implications of choice. Of course, this means that one should learn not
only to be skeptical of received ideas but to calculate one's own
advantages and interests in any situation. And indeed, there are
many in the university today who teach that "thinking for oneself" is essentially equivalent to calculating one's own self-interest.

Yet another school of thought, today often identified as "civic
republican" or "communitarian," finds such a conception of the
proper education of citizens absolutely appalling. To be sure, they
would encourage independent thinking, but to the end of public
judgment, not calculated self-interest.

Now when political theorists deliberate the necessary underpinnings of liberal democracy, they generally follow one of two approaches. The first tradition, which one might call "mechanical
liberalism," assumes that if one can create institutions that will
reliably transform self-interest and power-seeking into public interest, you can leave human nature pretty much as you find it. This
is the thought, of course, behind Adam Smith's idea of the market
and James Madison's conception of constitutional checks and balances. The second course is to postulate certain attitudes and dispositions that should be widespread in the populace if liberal
democratic government is to succeed. This is the spirit of much
pure democratic and civic republican theory today, and it obviously implies a very different conception of the education of citizens than the individualist model.[6]

What then would such a program of education look like? What
"habits of the heart" would it cultivate?[7] Here there is great uncertainty, and likely grave contentiousness, the closer one comes to a
level of detail sharper than platitude. Republican theorists speak of
developing "civic virtue." In the longer republican tradition, back
to Cicero, the virtues referred to specific dispositions of character.
Beyond public spiritedness, one might speak of such traits as pru-
dence, justice, magnanimity, seriousness, benevolence, and so on.
Precisely how one translates such ideals into an effective program
of education is unclear to me. I presume something more is required than moral suasion.

The most recent currents in liberal democratic theory stress the skills of reasoned deliberation as the heart of civic competence.[8] The aims of education might be to develop tolerance and understnding of diverse perspectives, the mutual search for common ground and a coherent conception of the common good, the faculty of critical examination of alternative policies and the justifications given for them. Some would associate this ideal with Jürgen Habermas' conception of "communicative competence."[9] In some versions, the process of reasoned deliberation is likened to scientific inquiry, and to the conception of practical reason that animates this essay.[10] But do not think I intend to resolve the question that easily.

The issue of course is that each statement of the aims of citizen education rests on a partisan position within the debate about the nature of liberal democratic politics itself. So the question inevitably arises of how we should make such a decision, and who should make it?

The matter seems manifestly political. Like the question of voting rights, or legislative powers, the program of citizen education is a *constitutive* quality of the regime, part of its underpinnings, and that seems obviously something for the people, ultimately, to decide. Still, to endorse this seemingly self-evident view puts us back in the awkward situation we encountered before. Is it our intent that the university teach the doctrine of education specified by the will of the people, without critical examination or independent interpretation of it, and that it shall *change* its doctrine as majority will changes?

Or, instead, is it the task of the university to deliberate the options and recommend a version of liberalism as public philosophy? Astounding as this sounds, perhaps it is. What else can be the purpose of the unceasing criticism of rival theories, the endless scrutiny of texts, but to attest in the end that some ideas of public purpose, some philosophic propositions about the quest for the common good, are more serviceable than others, and more appropriate to the education of citizens? If the purpose of the university is to exercise a kind of quality control in the realm of ideas, why should *political* ideas be excluded from its agenda?

The fundamental tension is still apparent. Each of these answers seems oddly in order, yet each is clearly suspect, and unacceptable as it stands. And no way of resolving the tension is yet in view.

Thus, we must return to the fundamental question. Can the education of citizens (with citizenship narrowly conceived as having to do only with the formally public, or political, life of society) define the educational mission of the university? Is the university competent to provide a liberal education, if that means an education for liberals? Can it do so with integrity?

Utility

While political and moral philosophers seem preoccupied with the public life, for most people the tasks of this formal, exclusively political citizenship are but a small, often a trivial, engagement. Our social contribution lies more in other realms of activity, in family, in community, in vocation. Students still say, persistently, that their main reason for going to college is to prepare for a career.[11] Perhaps the development and transmission of useful skills is the basic public purpose of the university.[12]

There is a broad public expectation that the universities will teach the young how to earn a living. It is also understood that the universities are a primary instrument of social mobility. This is how one moves up and out. For many today, higher education serves the same purposes that immigration did two generations ago.

The public expects the universities to enable people to better themselves, in down-to-earth, cash-value terms. But do we really mean to imply that the *aim* of education should be to enable some to gain greater wealth or rise in social rank? Is not this but a by-product of the actual good we seek, which is to invest people with the competence to perform well in various callings and professions?

But if this is the case, who is going to decide what it means to do a particular job well? Is this something the public is entitled to define? Or is this a matter for the academic experts?

It has long been customary to distinguish between "liberal" and "practical" or "vocational" education. It is said that a liberal education is something one pursues for its own sake, not for instrumental value.[13] However, advocates of liberal education have long stressed its utility. Even John Henry Cardinal Newman, that rigorous apostle of the classic ideal of liberal studies, insisted that liberal education meant the development of those capabilities of mind that could be applied to any calling.[14] Today we say that a liberal education prepares people to learn with discernment and judgment, at once to see broadly and to penetrate to the heart of matters, all traits essential in a complex and fast-changing world, where specific specialized training quickly becomes obsolete and limiting.

Nonetheless, specialized professional education is the very essence of the contemporary university. Every program of study, no matter how "liberal," culminates in a major. Perhaps the central commitment of the university, the single activity that gives it clear identity, is to the sustained examination of established doctrine and technique, to the end of enhancing some form of human performance.

However, professional education is obviously not just a matter of learning to follow the "steps" of prescribed technique. Professional education is always a subtle and sensitive, and somewhat elusive, process. It is a matter of evoking dispositions to perceive and interpret in a certain way. It is also learning to judge and to act according to a system of ideals, norms, and standards. Professional education is always moral education. It is a process of induction into a normative culture, a way of life, an order whose code is justified as contributing to excellence in the performance of a vital human function. This is, or ought to be, the tone of education in agriculture, forestry, or journalism, in law, medicine, or preparation for any of the learned professions.

Who then shall prescribe the normative order of a profession? Who shall define how much foresters shall think of cost-effectiveness and how much sustainability, how doctors shall deal with the dying, how political scientists should teach in the face of fundamental controversy—or, God help us, what integrity should mean in advertising, marketing, or corporate finance? Is it up to the university itself to scrutinize its programs, and certify that indeed all its teachings represent best practice? Or should the elders of the various professions define the norms, and is it up to the university to educate according to their will? Or is it for us, the people, to decide what the working code of those who provide us with the most fundamental services is to be? Who has the right to make such decisions? And then, who indeed *is* going to guard the guardians?

The tantalizing question, of course, is whether there are *general* principles that can be used to take the measure of any profession, or whether each professional code is unique. Is good husbandry in agriculture at all like objectivity and fairness in journalism, or good design in civil engineering or architecture? Are such ideas latent, intimated, in the general code of inquiry that unifies and animates the university?

If we could identify the common grounds of responsible performance, we would have not only a basis for appraisal of the teachings of the university but the foundations for a philosophy of liberal education as well. The point, reaffirming Newman's appeal of a century ago, would be to teach those dispositions of mind and soul that are common to all callings.

This is an ideal of liberal education far more bewitching than the dull discussions of six hours of this and six hours of that which now seem about all that animates our conception of the core curriculum.[15] But do we have the slightest idea of what such an ideal would look like, translated into practice? Is the university competent to teach practical reason? Can it do so with integrity?

Character

It is often said that education should aim not just at intellectual training but at the development of the "whole person." I have intimated that education either for citizenship or for a profession must have something to do, if we take it seriously, with traits of character. As Aristotle would have had it, our sense of what it takes to achieve excellence in a craft or calling, or as a citizen, is related to our sense of what it takes to be a good person.[16] Allan Bloom's lament for the "closing of the American mind" was based on concern not for loss of skill, but for the qualities that our institutions of higher education would be committed to cultivating.[17]

Do we then expect the university to nurture specific traits of character? If so, which ones? Which fundamental dispositions is a liberally educated person supposed to exhibit? Is it intellectual autonomy and skepticism that we wish to foster? Or tolerance of diversity? Or social activism? Or scientific detachment? Or breadth of interests? The university is a bully pulpit, and its char-

acter-shaping aspirations mingle perilously with various political
agendas. Perhaps what is really at issue in the logrolling negotia-
tions over the core curriculum is whether students shall be exposed to one course in consciousness-raising, one in scientific objectivity, and one in respect for traditional values. The crucial
question, and it is one to which we shall return, is how the university could justify any particular effort to shape the qualities of
the soul.

Why Classic Definitions Fail

Again, what is it that we expect the university to do? How should
students be different four—or eight—years later? How do we expect the human mind and spirit to be transformed? How will we
know if the university has succeeded or failed?

We have surveyed certain classic definitions of the aims of liberal
education. This is the eternal stuff of commencement addresses
and elevating essays. But in the end we are not going to take it
seriously. If someone actually set out to *accomplish* one of these
purposes, efficiently and single-mindedly, all would be tumult and
protest. We would object first, I think, because of an inherent
sense of balance, that pursuing any one of these objectives would
jeopardize some larger, not yet articulate, sense of mission. But
we would also back off, I believe, because we are not sure that the
university is competent to decide, and therefore to teach, these
things. Does the university *know* the qualities of a liberally educated person? Of a citizen? Of a doctor, officer, or *scientist* for that
matter? Thus we have to relate the public, the educational, function of the university to its intrinsic purpose, its role in inquiry.
As we shall quickly see, this is a more complicated issue than it
first appears. What do we expect the university to *know?* What do
we expect it to be able to *find out?* Only when we put answers to
these questions together with those that concern educational purpose can we begin to come to grips with the problem of what the
university can be expected to teach with integrity, and thus find a
ground for appraising its performance.

The Intrinsic Purpose of the University

The intrinsic purpose of the university is to find out what can be
done with the powers of mind. Over the centuries, this project has

taken different forms; it has led in diverse directions. We have tried
to capture the underlying logic of the universe. We have aimed at
making sense of nature and discerning the intentions of God. We
have created artifacts of pure reason, such as mathematics. We
have scrutinized our own techniques—our arts and crafts, our institutions, our law—to see if we could make them better by thinking them through. And we have tried to reflect on our power of
thought itself, to see if by understanding *this* we could begin to
get a grip on our destiny.

All of this has long been acknowledged to be the essential, routine, everyday work of the university. The emphases, of course,
shift from time to time. However, I do not want to make too
much of the great philosophic epochs and controversies that have
marked the passing ages, the Enlightenment repudiation of Scholasticism, the issues between rationalism and romanticism, the disputes of our century over the continued vitality of the project of
scientific understanding. From my perspective, these are but arguments within the trade, within the family. More important here
are the long continuities. There is a remarkable thread of shared
expectations that links the medieval and the modern university.
Similarly, the general sense in society of what universities are supposed to do has certainly been as stable as our sense of the purpose
of any other social institution. The *idea* of the university has surely
been at least as consistent as the idea of the state, or the business
corporation, or the church, or the guild, or the family.

Part of the task of the university, one supposes, is to tell us what
it *knows*. The university knows the date of the Treaty of Ghent,
the chemical properties of manganese, and the laws of Newton. It
has a copy of Plato's *Republic,* and it can tell you about the Sioux
Ghost Dance and the federal tax code. It can identify the bug in
your garden and the tree on your lawn.

We can picture the university as a place where people go out on
voyages of discovery and return to tell us what they have found.
They peer through telescopes and microscopes, they pour through
forgotten manuscripts, and then they report on their "findings."
It is as though the university were a great bazaar filled with exotic
wares from faraway places. The university trades in *uncommon*
knowledge. It tells us how things are outside the immediate local-
ity, beyond the boundaries of the commonplace and common
sense.

This is a sound and conventional view of the function of the university, and it accounts, I think, for much of what the university does in practice. But, we already suspect, this cannot be the whole of it. There must be more to the story.

Let us try again. We do not expect the university to present us with brute facts, simply to *show* us distant galaxies, *report* that microbes exist, and *relate* the story of the Thirty Years War. This is not the point at all. It is not what the university *knows* but what it *means* that matters. It is the work of the university to *interpret* the facts: to spin a web of relations of cause and effect, of point and purpose, to give a *reason* for what it thinks is going on in the world. The real aim of the institution is to provide *understanding,* to produce theory, philosophy, theology, and perhaps—when that fails or before it is ready—poetry.

But now the matter becomes distinctly sticky. We expect the university to tell us what it all means but we do not really believe that it knows. It can teach Darwinian biology, Big Bang cosmology, the way Max Weber looked at authority or Marx at history. This is fascinating stuff indeed, and we come to grasp how such theories can pull together a wide range of phenomena and, somehow, explain. But we are too sophisticated—and the university insists that we be so sophisticated—to think of any of these frameworks as absolutely true, in the most serious sense of the term. We know perfectly well that the university does not know "what it's all about." And the university, as part of its most fundamental credo, must profess that it does not. It is guessing, just like the rest of us.

So what is the function of the university? Is it to provide surmise, speculation, and conjecture? Is its purpose to respond to our curiosity and wonder though it cannot, by its own admission, satisfy it? Are the universities simply the seers and saga tellers of a later age? Some think so, but their attitude is idiosyncratic.[18] We have not yet gotten a satisfactory answer to our question of what the university fundamentally and intrinsically should be able to do.

It is not what the university knows but how it finds out that matters. The task of the university is to find out what can be done with the powers of reason. Its real work is to produce useful *ways* of thinking. The only reason why the knowledge taught by the university has any special standing (why it is better than ordinary impression or the views promoted by other institutions—including the state and the church) rests not on the nature of *what* is taught but on the process that produced it.

So the essential task of the university is to manufacture ways of thinking—habits, techniques, disciplines of reason. This is the thesis I now introduce to guide our inquiry: to find out where it leads. There will be room enough and time to examine its implications thoroughly. We will test it against competing perspectives. We will deliberate it, correct it, and perfect it if we can.

Thought, as we all know, in its natural state is in constant flux. It is random, errant, hit-or-miss, disorderly. The ruminations of the mind run free. The purpose of the university then is to build structures of thought, systems of reason that are dependable, that will yield good results whenever we put them into practice. The function of the university is to capture the fleeting ideas that work best. It is said that architecture is frozen music. By the same token, the disciplines of reason are frozen thought.

All of this depends on the peculiar human capacity to *learn:* to follow a pattern of thinking so that we can reach a certain result, and then to reflect on the adequacy of that result, and adjust and correct the process of thinking so that we can do better next time. This process of controlled thought, of thinking according to a system, is what we call reason.

The process of thought is open, unpredictable, unbounded. We can never define the limits or the possibilities of mind. For this reason, the products of the university are always imperfect and provisional. Oddly, we recognize that the possibilities of thought are not defined by formal axiomatic systems of reason but that we can, through thinking, recognize its limits and distortions. The moral of this, of course, is that the university always understands its teaching as improvised, that it always keeps working on its schemes of reason, never entrench them as dogma.

The basic work of the university is to create systems of reason, practices of inquiry. This does not mean that the knowledge taught by the university is unimportant. Anyone born in this era should know the size of the universe and the age of the earth, as we now imagine them to be. This is the great mystery wisdom of our age, and these are the "current findings" of the disciplines of astronomy and geology. But equally as wondrous as are these "facts" is the process by which we arrived at them. In the end, the only reason we have to believe that the knowledge is sound is the nature of the process by which it was discovered.

This proposition of mine, that the essential purpose of the university is to develop methods of thinking, seems consistent with the dominant epistemologies, the theories of knowledge in our century. The standard belief is no longer that we apprehend the world directly, through "sensations" (as was held by classic empiricism). Nor, generally, do we think our systems of reason sheer fantasy, with no connection to the world. (However, as we shall see, there is a fashionable wave in current thought—postmodernists, Nietzscheans, sociologists of knowledge—that seems to think precisely that.) My position is that our knowledge rests on an *interaction* between mind and the world. This is the basic tenet of most contemporary scientific rationalism. More broadly, it is the position of philosophic pragmatism. But as we shall see, it is not an uncontestable position.

All the university can teach then is what it has figured out so far: the ideas that seem to work in practice. We teach the ideas we think best correspond to the workings of the world (if we are talking natural science—or theology) and those that seem to correspond best to the workings of the human mind and spirit (if we are talking philosophy, or politics, or economics, or ethics). And we teach the practical methods that seem to work best (if we are talking medicine, or engineering, or administration). We admit this is but a partial reality, an aspect of reality, probably a distorted reality, but it is the best we can do at the moment.

The Purpose of the University and the Enlightenment Project

We are probing the tension between the public and the inherent functions of the university, trying to see if this will bring us closer to an idea of its essential purpose. For all its claims to independence, the university has never stood aloof, isolated, from the society of which it was a part. It has taken its cues from the civilization around it, inquired into it, even as it contributed to the unfolding of that civilization.

The university, by its very nature, has a public role to play. It is an *educational* institution. As such, it is expected to have an impact on the society of which it is a part. Its activities are not simply self-referential. We, the citizens, then quite properly have an interest in the performance of the university; we are entitled to deliberate its aims and purposes, to frame a conception of what we expect it to do. But I have also argued that the mission of the university cannot be understood simply as an act of public will. The university has an inherent function: to explore the possibilities of mind. Our public expectations for the educational mission of the university must be consistent with this core commitment of the institution. Else we will recognize them as unsuitable, corrupt.

The real work of the university is to enhance the powers of mind. Now, immediately, we see the relation of research and teaching in new perspective. It is not only the "results" of inquiry—the facts and theories—that the university should teach. Rather, the very *object* of inquiry should be to find out how thought can do better. The core educational aim of the university then is to teach those thoughtways, those habits of mind, that it can show work well in comprehending the world and deciding what to do in it. And it is understood—but as a pure act of faith—not only that the ways of thinking taught by the university bear on the further advance of scholarship and science but that they lead us to think clearly and carefully about all the affairs of everyday life.

All of this may seem quite sane and sensible. In fact, it is a position with momentous and disturbing overtones. It is to declare that the ways of the university ought to become the ways of the world. It is to accept the full force of the Enlightenment project.

To accept this argument is to say that the habits of thought of the scholar and scientist should also be the habits of thought of the good citizen and the good professional. The argument is as old as Plato and Aristotle, as new as Dewey and any number of current liberal democratic theorists. To teach the dispositions of sound inquiry is also to teach the dispositions of good reason. Furthermore, the task of the university is not only to explore, systematically, the nature of the world, but also to scrutinize the practices of everyday life to see if they can be improved. The aim of political science is to improve the conduct of government. That of home economics, to make the management of the household more intelligent. The improvement of practical reason implies not only disseminating the habits of thought of the university but applying them to all forms of organized social activity.

Still, it takes an enormous act of faith to assume that the paths of science and scholarship and those of the good society will inevitably converge, that an invisible hand will automatically guide the university to promote those modes of reason that will best enhance and perfect the civilization.

Not everyone will subscribe unreservedly to the proposition. Today, as throughout the past three centuries, many try to resist the overwhelming force of rationalism. In the name of religion, or traditional ties of clan or ethnicity, many, often at great price and peril, try to insulate themselves from the threat that the spirit of rational analysis, the temper of mind and heart taught by the university, will insinuate itself into every corner of everyday life.

So it is apparent that the tension between the public and intrinsic functions of the university is still with us. I have not at a stroke, with a single declaration, solved all the problems. We are still steering by intimations and approximations. It remains pertinent for citizens to ask whether the university teaches what the public ought to know. It is also pertinent for the university to ask whether it is competent to teach what the people expects. It is also in order for citizens to ask for the warrants for the university's teaching, for a clear justification of why its methods may be presumed to be *better* methods. This uneasy tension is the very basis of rational deliberation. And all of this takes us very far from the easier solutions: the university as totally independent in its quest for truth by virtue of the right of academic freedom; the university as free-form marketplace of ideas; the university as simple instrument of democratic will.

CHAPTER FOUR

Competence: What Can We Know? What Are We Entitled to Teach?

Certainly, we do not want the university to teach indiscriminately all the varied meanderings of the mind. We expect it to sort out the better from the worse ideas, to teach the more reliable habits of thought. To put the point as belligerently as possible, we expect the university to teach the truth, and the paths to truth, and to denounce deception, spuriousness, illusion, and error. This implies, of course, that the university knows in what direction truth lies. And for a generation as skeptical and sophisticated as our own, all of this is awkward doctrine. We don't talk much about truth and falsity any more.

Nonetheless, the university must be able to give a rational defense of its teachings, of the standards it uses to distinguish what is worthy of being taught from what is not. In a liberal democracy, acts of public authority must be justified. Those in positions of power have no right to do just as they please, whimsically or arbitrarily. They must give good reasons for their decisions, reasons of law or principle.[1] Now, implicitly, we vest the university with the authority to set the rules of truth-seeking for the society. We expect it to prescribe the preferred methods of reason, perhaps of sensitivity. The university has a public character and it must be able to account publicly for its acts.[2] It is the *strength* of that account, that justification, which will establish the legitimacy of the university in a free society. And all of this seems to imply that the university must endorse some tenable epistemology, a theory of knowledge. If our educational program is to make sense, if it is to be responsible, we have to proceed according to some conception of what thought is capable of doing and what it is not, and what it can become at the height of its powers. And these, of course, have been among the most contentious questions of philosophy through all the ages.

Thus Plato taught that the mind works through intimations of timeless forms, imperfectly perceived, and he did *not* teach that the human mind (not even the mind of Socrates) could grasp the form itself. Aristotle, while sharing Plato's view that there was a realm of ordered being that eluded mind, nonetheless thought that reason could penetrate further, that by asking the right questions about the principle of development, the force of growth or change within a creature, a natural process, or a human activity, we could learn something of the true design of nature, and how to harmonize human conduct with it. The Christians stressed the point that whatever reason could teach us about the Creation, about present, earthly, things, it was inadequate to know the actual purposes of God. That required faith—and grace.

The Enlightenment philosophers had great confidence in the power of reason to know the world. Descartes assumed that we could trust our "clear and distinct" ideas, for God was no deceiver. The British empiricists thought the mind was best understood as an apparatus that registered "sensations" pretty accurately from external reality. But Kant insisted that the mind stamped its own categories on the world and hence we could not know it "in essence," or as it really was. Hegel presumed that the whole point of history was the effort of mind to grasp reality, while diverse skeptics, romantics, and followers of Nietzsche proclaimed that the mind made up its own reality, and there was no way of knowing whether thought could mirror the world. And so it has gone, throughout most of the past two and a half millennia.

Now, as a practical matter, the university is going to have to have some policy about all this. It is going to have to endorse some idea of the known and the knowable if it is going to go about its business at all. To be sure, actually proclaiming, as a corporate body, on matters philosophic is the last thing the university wants to do these days, but the issue is unavoidable. We are going to have to decide what we can teach with integrity and what we can not.

In the previous chapter, I asked which conceptions of educational purpose the university could teach with integrity. Here I reverse the process and ask whether any of the conventional tests of knowledge and the knowable could yield an acceptable program of education. I hope to show that they would not. My purpose in all of this is to suggest that the answer to our quest cannot be found by following any of the prepared positions of the day. I think we are going to have to go beyond current assumptions and try a new approach.

Reliable Knowledge

Again, the American university was intentionally designed as a knowledge factory. Its purpose was the production of durable, trustworthy ideas through systematic, organized inquiry. It might seem then that what the university has a right to teach with authority are the products of this process, those thoughts that have been checked and rechecked, examined from every angle and certified sound.

One of the liveliest, and here most pertinent, philosophic debates of recent years has been over the "demarcation criterion," over what is to count as scientific knowledge and what is not. It has become clear that to ask that a statement be "verified"—proven true—is to ask too much. Nothing is indubitable, rationally certain in the strictest sense, and to insist on this as the criterion of knowledge is to put the whole enterprise of rational inquiry in doubt, to open the door to all forms of irrationalism and nihilism. Science, Peirce insisted, must always keep its own fallibility in mind, and it must never "close the door to further inquiry."[3] Thus, Karl Popper suggested that the appropriate test of a scientific statement was that it had resisted repeated efforts to find it false.[4] More generally, the current view is that scientific knowledge is that which has been sustained through rigorous critical examination according to the rules, procedures, and methods of a community governed by the critical, self-corrective methods of scientific inquiry.[5]

Now I think it is a very common view that what the university ought to teach is knowledge it can show to be correct, methods it can demonstrate to get results. The purpose of the university is to separate the wheat from the chaff; hence the aim of education is to disseminate the more trustworthy thoughts. We seem to expect all disciplines to work the way we fervently hope the medical school does: that what is passed along is carefully considered best practice, the most prudent, responsible, and dependable approach, the right thing to do in a given situation.

The official position is that what the university *should* teach is its fund of reliable knowledge. It should *not* teach whimsy, supposition, superstition, fable, or fraud. On this account, the fundamental purpose of liberal education is to bring the student to understand the core of fundamental agreed-upon knowledge about the world and the works of humanity, and the methods by which this knowledge was won.

But the moment it is stated baldly, the utter insufficiency of such a rule for deciding what should and should not be taught becomes apparent. The stratum of reliable knowledge on which there is reasonable consensus is remarkably thin in any field. It is not rich enough to sustain the life of the mind. In physics, the foundation of classical mechanics is little more than the point of departure for the remarkable—and highly contentious—flowering of speculative thought about the ultimate properties of matter, and the cosmos, that has developed in recent years. In my own field, political science, there may be some general agreement on the descriptive characteristics of governments, but on very little else. Those disciplines that really seem to have the most settled doctrine are generally those that have been intellectually quite dead for a substantial period of time or those that have achieved rigor by systematically excluding everything from their domain that does not fit perfectly with the dominant paradigm.

If we really accepted the test of reliable knowledge as a criterion for establishing what should and should not be taught, what kind of education would we have? Do we really want to teach as though there were no doubt or confusion, and no inklings, hunches, or visions either?

A strict interpretation of the standard principle would require the university to show that its teachings have passed scrutiny. They are consensually endorsed by the learned professions. They have been found trustworthy. But the lifeblood of the *activity* of inquiry is not so much consensus as contention. The vitality of a discipline depends on the power of its settled doctrine, to be sure, but also on its disputed interpretations, rival positions, problems, anomalies, and confusions. The intellectual *importance* of a field lies in part in what it can assert with assurance, but it also may come from its *ignorance,* its manifest inability to account for the most important questions in its domain. (Consider either oncology or theology in this regard.)

In the face of academic controversy and uncertainty, what is the appropriate pedagogy? Gerald Graff, reflecting on the stormy battles of the contemporary humanities—the disputes over the canon and among the various schools of criticism—recommends that we "teach the argument."[6] This sounds promising. Academic integrity should require that we be very explicit about the exact level of confidence we have in our statements. Where there are contradictory theories or evidence, that should be made clear. Where we are collectively confused about fundamentals, all we have to teach are points of view.

But note carefully: if we make "teaching the argument" the actual rationale of our efforts, our concept of the purpose of education shifts subtly but certainly. Now the main object is to teach not so much the *fruits* of inquiry as the *process* of inquiry. The aim in teaching geology becomes that students understand not so much the evolution of the earth as how geologists have come to think about the earth as they do, and how they quarrel about their understanding. The point of political science is to learn not about politics but how political scientists think—and argue—about politics. The test of integrity in teaching if we take this line is not so much that it transmits reliable knowledge as that it fairly represents the "state of mind" of a discipline at a certain point in its development.

This is a way out of epistemological peril. It sounds good. It seems consistent with our earlier insistence on the primacy of method over sheer information. But think carefully. Is this really the solution we seek? Here we come to see clearly the very real distinction between the goal of teaching practical reason and that of teaching academic reason, pure and simple. Just a bit earlier, at the end of Chapter 2, we came upon this very same problem, but from a different angle, when we asked whether we really wanted to teach students to be detached observers rather than participants.

Is it more important that a liberally educated person know what goes on in the university or what goes on in the world? Do we truly suppose that it is the mark of the liberally educated person to know the rival schools of criticism but perhaps not the great works of literature, to know the varied techniques of economic modeling but not the functions of the Federal Reserve Board? It increasingly seems from our practice that this is our intent. Granted, it is important that budding academics catch up on the argument. But the preparation of professional scholars, the simple reproduction of the disciplines, cannot be the decisive concern.

It seems eminently more important to teach the practices of actual human activities than merely those of the learned professions. But this is to presume that we can teach reliably about the methods and the motives, the purposes and the processes, of the world out there, that we can teach about the polity and the economy and not just about political science and economics, that we can teach ways of reason that work dependably in the actual encounters and confrontations of life, and not just in academic disputation. And that, of course, is precisely what is at issue. If the university does not have some clear, sound, dependable grasp of how the world works and what works in the world, why is it entitled to teach at all?

Still, in the face of academic controversy, we must all, to some extent, "teach the argument." But what test of integrity does *this* imply? Is the rule that dissident voices are to be heard only when the discipline concurs that all are respectable? That sounds dangerously restrictive. Is the rule that we should teach everything that makes its presence felt—anything that happens to get published? That puts the latest cult fad for communicating with extraterrestrial beings right up there with astronomy. Granted, much of what *is* taught is merely fashionable rather than reliable. And many instructors choose texts simply to be "provocative," which means they consciously teach what is generally regarded as sensationalist, exaggerated, or wrong. Again, how do we decide, collectively as well as individually, which intellectual positions are worthy of transmission and which are not? Sometimes the issues are monumental. Consider: should biologists, as a matter of course, teach Teilhard de Chardin's *The Phenomenon of Man* alongside standard Darwinian doctrine? If so, why? If not, why not?

Still, it might be argued that what distinguishes *quality* in higher education is that it brings students the most up-to-date views, the theories at the "cutting edge." The run-of-the-mill university can teach nothing but reliable knowledge and method, the interchangeable, standardized, textbook course. Only the great universities can take students to the brink of uncertainty. Is this not a compelling case for the merits of "teaching the argument"?

But the fact of the matter is that there is great risk and uncertainty, a high probability of error, at the cutting edge. The half-life of new ideas is amazingly short. Fashionable theories often deteriorate quickly. An education focused on current academic controversy, like one focused on current events, quickly tends to obsolescence. It comes to seem quaint and out of date. That was when we read *The Lonely Crowd,* learned political science behaviorism, studied Marxist economics, Skinnerian psychology, and argued Viet Nam. There is much to be said for grounding a liberal education in the big questions and the perennial concerns, perhaps in those topics and texts which have become classic, that have stood the test of time. Now all we have to know is which are the big questions, which the perennial concerns, what is a classic, and why the rules of reason of bygone ages should be the most pertinent today.

We are searching for a rule that would justify the university's presumption to distinguish the better from the worse understanding, the more and less penetrating habits of thought. Yet the exercise so far leaves us strangely dissatisfied. Surely there is more to liberal education than the mere transmission of certified knowledge or induction into the ways of the learned professions. Where do wondering, provocation, bafflement, being stymied, figuring out, judging calmly, and seeing clearly fit in? There is obviously more to it than can be contained in the philosophy explicated so far. Yet these are the clear implications of the standard doctrine of what is to count as knowledge and what is not. Once again, we discern the tension between the public, the educational function of the university and its intrinsic mission of inquiry.

Nonetheless, the standard rule is not the only test of ideas alive in the university today. It is strongly contested by other theories of the known and the knowable. Let us consider where such rival epistemologies might take us if they were used as a guide to educational purpose.

Perspectivism

There are a variety of reasons for teaching diverse perspective rather than settled knowledge.

The first, we have already noted, is simple intellectual candor. We acknowledge the uncertainty and equivocation of a discipline. We are willing to let students see what goes on behind the scenes, in the sausage factory.

We may, however, also want to make clear precisely how the problem of truth arises. There is, of course, an inevitable subjective element in thought. We see things differently, depending on our situation, our expectations, and our interests. Now it is this very awareness of diverse perspective that makes inquiry possible—and necessary. The fact of subjectivity leads us to ask whether it is possible that one or the other of us is mistaken, or whether we are looking at different aspects of the same thing. In that case, by coordinating our efforts, and sharing information, we may come closer to an understanding of what reality is really like. Or we may simply come to understand, in wonder, that we can *suspect* much more about the meaning of the world than we can ever hope to demonstrate to one another.

But the crucial point is that it is only when we are *faced* with diverse perspectives that we have to ask which idea is better, which we should accept and act upon, which is to say, which is closer to the truth, or the essential purpose we seek. The question never arises when we are locked in a culture of certainty. Such problems, and thus philosophy, seem to arise most easily in the port and crossroad cities—Athens, Amsterdam—as they do today in the university towns, where ideas and cultures clash. They would not come up, say, in the heart of Imperial China or Aztec Mexico.[7]

There is nothing particularly surprising—or threatening—about this. As Juliana Hunt points out, subjectivity may change the way the world looks, but it does not change the world. Conversely, objectivity limits what there is to see, but it does not determine how the mind will see it. As long as one takes it for granted that subjectivity and objectivity are intrinsically related, that this is the natural rhythm of thought, there is nothing in the distinction between them to be particularly concerned about.[8] The trouble begins when it is supposed that subjectivity means that we cannot know the object at all, or that the reality of the objective must at all cost be defended against subjective distortion. And it is precisely along these categoric, winner-take-all lines that the battle over what the university can presume to teach with integrity has come to be waged.

Radical Relativism

The guiding premise of one doctrine taught by the contemporary university is that the mind cannot know the world at all.

Everything we suppose about what is going on "out there" is distorted by cultural assumptions, frameworks of ideas, the nature of language, and the quirks and categories inherent in the nature of the mind itself. We can *see* only with this totally inadequate intellectual apparatus. Furthermore, it is a wild leap of faith to presume that the world *has* meaning to be discerned. For all we know, all *is* chance, randomness, at best statistical probability. So what we are doing is not discovering meaning but bravely imputing meaning to a universe which, more likely than not, has none.

Thus, our systems of thought are best understood as akin to stories or fables. They are the myths through which we interpret the world, and they are not different in kind from the myths of peoples untouched by science and rationalism. On the question of creation, there is little to choose between the Big Bang, Genesis, and the Tree of Ydrigisal. Our theories are artifacts of language, and language is fundamentally metaphorical. It does not mirror objective reality. Rather, such cognitive structures are poetic visions, and such visions are incommensurable and incomparable. There is no sense asking which is more trustworthy, or for that matter, ennobling, for there are no rational standards that would enable us to adjudicate among them.

The university then is engaged not in a progressive process of building reliable knowledge, patiently distinguishing the more from the less tenable patterns of thought. It is rather simply another participant in the conversation of humanity, in which we can do no more than exchange impressions of how things seem to us.[9] Systems of ideas succeed one another, not because some give a more adequate depiction of the world, but just because they "catch on," or are found more fascinating. Richard Rorty, one of the more extreme protagonists of this point of view, says, "Once one found out what could be done with a Galilean vocabulary, nobody was interested in doing the things that used to be done . . . with an Aristotelian one."[10]

One might suppose that such a theory of knowledge would yield a free-spirited pedagogy, a view of educational purpose that would stress creativity and personal expression with scant regard for rules of evidence, rational rigor, or corrigibility. Yet strangely, this utter subjectivism frequently leads to a tightly drawn picture of appropriate method. For on this understanding, the very point of inquiry is to *reveal* the contingency of all systems of thought.

The appropriate stance of the intellect is *outside* established disciplines of reason. One does not approach the work of the mind as party to an ongoing project: as physicist, or pediatrician, or Catholic, or liberal. The object of analysis is not to *use* structures of reason but to *account* for them, as one would any other phenomenon in the brute, pointless reality "out there."

Thus, strangely, this exaggerated relativism comes to mesh with, and reinforce, that tone of dispassionate objectivity that the contemporary university seems so intent on nurturing. Again, the clear intimation is that one should approach the world as observer, as spectator.

Historically, the idea that analysis implied primarily precise, dispassionate observation was most closely associated with the sciences. But this new methodological imperative for the study of ideas emerges from, of all places, literature. The premise is that all systems of thought, whatever their form, whether science, or law, or art, or institutions, are to be regarded metaphorically as texts. And a text is, after all, an object, out there in the world. It is a phenomenon one encounters and tries to figure out, like a canyon, or St. Elmo's fire, or background radiation. A text is said to have no inherent meaning. It must be given one, through the process of interpretation. Like other forms of reductionist science, a text cannot be explained in its own terms but only in relation to something more fundamental, more "real." Thus, as the physicist must reduce all explanations to ideas of force and motion, energy and matter, or the biologist to organic development, so the critical analyst must show how systems of reason sustain relationships of power.

The object of inquiry then is to demonstrate how systems of reason reinforce patterns of dominance and submission, how they "normalize" people, adjust them to the imperatives of social order. Ideas are to be understood, fundamentally, in their political aspect. In recent years, this mode of analysis is most prominently associated with the postmodernist philosophers: Michel Foucault, Jacques Derrida, and others. It is also apparent in the critical legal studies movement and in what is sometimes called the rhetoric of the human sciences. However, these recently fashionable approaches all bear a striking resemblance to the project that used to be called the sociology of knowledge, its roots in the likes of Karl Marx, Max Weber, and Karl Mannheim. There the object was to explain systematic thought, science, theory, as ideology, as a "social construction of reality."[11] In all such approaches, the idea of self-reflection does not mean the deliberate clarification of aims and objectives, of what one seeks to know or to do well, as it is in practical reason. Rather, one tries to discover the "determinants" of one's thought in the social forces that are said to be the ultimate sources of the dispositions of the mind.

For these schools of thought, an analysis succeeds if it demonstrates how a theoretical apparatus is part of the phenomenology of power. This is the crucial standard, the test of the sounder and more significant analysis, and thus the criterion which separates what is worth teaching and what is not.

On this account, it is then a *mistake* to teach chemistry, or law, or political economy, "just as it is," guilelessly, as though such disciplines had an identity and purpose of their own. To do so is to teach *error,* to participate, wittingly or not, in the perpetuation of a system of suppression of authentic thought. To teach truly is to teach critically, to demonstrate how the disciplines serve the large arbitrary, since contingent, framework of social control.

What conception of educational purpose flows from this image of the known and the knowable? The manifest aim is to "liberate" the mind from preconception and distortion, to set it free so that it might act autonomously and authentically, decide for itself how things truly are, interpret the world on its own.

If all systems of thought are contingent, if knowledge is essentially subjective, then it might seem that the basing point of education would be to come to "know oneself." One asks how one "feels" about things and through a raised consciousness comes to realize how one's awareness has been warped and thwarted by repressive ideas and institutions. Education would be the cultivation of personal expression, sensitivity, tolerance. The aims would be vaguely therapeutic, in the Freudian sense.

To celebrate creativity and sensitivity is not, of course, a bad thing in itself. It has a place in a philosophy of education. But an education founded in critical analysis will not do this, for it fosters, in the end, an unvarying suspicion of all patterns of ideas, including those of the apparently unfettered mind.

In this philosophy, the mark of the educated person would seem to be skeptical estrangement from all patterns of rationality, all organized systems of inquiry, or worship, or collective effort, all consciously contrived communities or projects. The person who truly knows what is going on must renounce faith, loyalty, and dedication to a cause. The authentic personality must stand quite alone, outside any organized human endeavor.

Now, in a ghastly sort of way, all of this might seem compatible with a certain image of liberal education. Classic liberalism, after all, invented the image of the individual in the state of nature who, unencumbered by ties of tradition or convention, could reason clearly and alone. The aim of liberal education, we have already noted, has long been to empower students to "think for themselves," to shake them out of the dogmatic slumbers of inherited belief or unexamined presupposition. It might seem then that contemporary critical theory is perfectly compatible with the longer aims of liberal education as a relativizing experience.

However, a crucial distinction is now in order. The aim of liberalism was never estrangement from the rational enterprise of humanity. To return, in thought experiment, to the state of nature was but a momentary retreat, a pause to regain perspective, prior to the social contract, a reaching out to establish deliberate solidarity and ties of common purpose. In this liberalism is quite unlike the spirit of critical theory, which denies all hope of finding shared meaning and rational commitment in the world.

The epistemological slogan of this extreme contemporary perspectivism is that modernity has failed. The Enlightenment, on their telling, taught that reason could find truth. But no rational system is unassailable. Therefore, all rational systems are equally tenable. There are no tests that can distinguish definitively the better from the worse course of reason.

For the protagonist of practical reason, this is bewildering doctrine. In these attacks on modernity, the university is made to seem still in thrall to the Cartesian project. But in fact the standard view of reliable knowledge, with all its pragmatic overtones of fallibilism, corrigibility, and the guarantees of the worth of ideas resting in the critical consensus of the community of inquiry, has nothing whatsoever to do with indisputable, axiomatic, Cartesian reason. The philosophical antifoundationalists seem to be fighting a long-forgotten battle. For practical reason, a way of thinking need not be shown to be irrefutably true to be considered rational. It just has to be shown to be better than the evident alternatives in pursuing some particular human purpose.

Clearly, the spirit of this extreme version of critical theory is precisely the reverse of that of practical reason. For this critical theory, the standpoint is *outside* a system of thought; the aim, to demonstrate its corruption. For practical reason, the position is *within* the rational enterprise. The aim is to learn to participate intelligently in an organized human project, to improve and perfect it if one can. These are, clearly, entirely contrary images of educational purpose.

Open-mindedness

Before going on, I must partially exempt one school of thought from this general fulmination against doctrinal relativism. I have argued, throughout, that the main business of the university is to teach reliable practices of thought. Yet there are those who protest that inquiry today must consciously resist prescriptive methodology. This is the position sometimes called, rather dramatically, intellectual anarchism; its most prominent spokesman is Paul Feyerabend.

Feyerabend's case is that science does not progress by rigid adherence to method. The rule that we build cumulatively, on the basis of established knowledge and method, inhibits scientific development. This condition preserves the *older* theory, not the better theory. Science should be open to the total range of thought, including long-discarded notions and those presently regarded as absurd. The only appropriate methodological maxim is *anything goes.*[12]

This view leads to a different idea of the competence of the university. Feyerabend argues that the state should not invest established disciplines with the right to prescribe curriculum and research priorities. The university should be an open marketplace of ideas. Scientific medicine should compete with witch doctors and faith healers; philosophers, presumably, with anyone who feels called to present a message about the meaning of life. Teaching and research decisions should be made not by academics but by democratically elected citizen panels.[13]

Feyerabend writes flamboyantly and his ideas are regarded as extreme. Still, on a certain reading, they are totally consistent with the spirit of my argument. Feyerabend points out that he regards his anarchism as a corrective to an excess of "law and order methodology." Were matters otherwise, he might argue the reverse.[14]

It is fundamental to practical reason that all aspects of an enterprise—including its fundamental presuppositions—be open to reflective reexamination. And it is probably true that most of the fundamental disciplines in the contemporary university have grown hidebound and rigid with age. In some parts of the university the fault may be intellectual promiscuity. In others it is dogmatic narrow-mindedness.

Feyerabend's anarchism seems intended to enhance the rationality of science as a practical enterprise. In contrast, the critical theorist sees science as just another story which has no special standing among the creations of the mind. Scientific revolutions occur, it is argued (now vastly misinterpreting Thomas Kuhn), not because later paradigms are more adequate but simply because a younger generation of scientists prevails as an older one dies off. Science is no more than rhetoric, persuasive speech. It is no more than another voice in the conversation of humanity, with no special standing or importance.[15]

To teach *this,* of course, is to define the point of education in a most peculiar way. But Feyerabend's point may be fair warning for a particular time and place. It is part of the discussion on the method appropriate to achieve more reliable understanding of the world. It is not an effort to prove that enterprise futile.

Classical Rationalism

The very structure of the contemporary university seems to presuppose a pluralist theory of knowledge. The free elective system seems to indicate that the university believes there are diverse approaches to knowledge and no necessary priority, or relationships, among them. There are some prerequisites and course sequences, to be sure, but no one infers from this that there is a kind of *natural* integration of the various fields of study. The curriculum itself suggests a resolute perspectivism, a firm belief that each subject is totally independent from its neighbors. There is no common metric by which their position in the total scheme of understanding is judged.

This seems to be the way the student experiences liberal education. One moves from class to class. No connecting threads are made manifest. One learns to turn on and turn off a certain style of discourse at hourly intervals. Now I think mathematically. Now I demonstrate Poe's inadequacies. Now I defend the autonomy of the state against critics. Nothing closer to sophistry can be imagined. The student's preeminent concern is to give the professors "what they want." One learns that it is highly inappropriate to use a language, or analytical approach, outside its intended context. John Kenneth Galbraith recounts the story of a fundamentalist student who took beginning economics from him. On the exam, Galbraith asked a question about the nature of money. The student responded that money was the root of all evil. Galbraith flunked him.[16]

It was otherwise in the classical university. Then there was presumed to be a necessary hierarchical relation among the subjects: some were derived from, dependent on the rest. In the medieval university theology was the queen of the disciplines. Following Aristotle, the natural distinction was between theoretical and practical knowledge. Metaphysics was the foundation of the theoretical sciences, which included physics (the study of change and development) and mathematics (the study of unchanging forms). Politics was the master practical science. Economics and ethics, for example, followed from deliberations about the polity. The trivium and quadrivium had parallel, but separate, foundations.

In America, the only clear alternative to the free elective system was some version of the classic liberal arts curriculum. The exemplar was long the "great books" program founded by Robert M. Hutchins at the University of Chicago.

Hutchins insisted that passage through an unrelated series of courses could not possibly constitute an education. He saw the creation of a coherent curriculum as a central *public* problem for the society:

> It is perhaps the highest function of the state to provide opportunities for the development of scholarship, the improvement of the professions, and the cultivation of the mind. It can only debase these objects and prevent their attainment if it permits the children of taxpayers to wander at will through the higher learning. Under these circumstances university degrees cease to have any meaning and universities, indeed, cease to exist.[17]

In his complaints about the free market American universities, Hutchins was but echoing objections raised a century earlier by John Henry Cardinal Newman about the perspectivism that had become the norm in British higher education.

Newman acknowledged that one had to acquire diverse forms of knowledge and see things from a variety of points of view. But this, in itself, could not be the end of education. The error of the university "has been the distraction and enfeebling of the mind by an unmeaning profusion of subjects; by implying that a smattering of a dozen branches of study is not shallowness, which it really is, but enlargement, which it is not."[18] One had to incorporate this fragmentary knowledge into an overriding system.

For Newman, the aim of learning diverse perspectives is a kind of opening up of vision, and it perhaps leads students to look back on earlier sureties and simplicities "with a sort of contempt and indignation, as if they were but fools, and the dupes of imposture."[19]

But this is not enough to constitute an education. The division of labor of the university, its specialized fields, must be based on some general philosophy, some idea of the unity of knowledge. A person who does not come to understand the overall system, "has no standard of judgment at all, and no landmarks to lead him to a conclusion."[20]

The aim of education is that people come to *evaluate* perspectives and diverse bodies of knowledge, that they apply thought or reason to the discrete elements of knowledge they have learned. "I say then, if we would improve the intellect, first of all we must ascend; we cannot gain real knowledge on a level; we must generalize, we must reduce to method, we must have a grasp of principles."[21]

All of this presumes that there *is* a unity to knowledge. In the contemporary university, this is not, shall we say, taken for granted. But those who believe that liberal education can be presented as a coherent program must, I think, have some such belief. Hutchins certainly did:

> Education implies teaching. Teaching implies knowledge. Knowledge is truth. The truth is everywhere the same. Hence education should be everywhere the same. . . . I suggest that the heart of any course of studies designed for the whole people will be, if education is rightly understood, the same at any time, in any place, under any political, social or economic conditions.[22]

As with Newman, Hutchins thought that liberal education unfolded according to orderly pattern, ascending from the particular to the more general studies, culminating in the capacity for philosophic reflection.[23]

Now to assume that liberal education should teach the unity of reason and knowledge implies that there is a unity to reason and knowledge, and that is today a most disputable proposition. Newman and Hutchins can defend an integrated ideal of liberal education because they fundamentally endorse an Aristotelian ideal of reason. Such a notion of liberal education is coherent because Aristotle's thought is coherent, and it is precisely the unity of Aristotle's teachings that have made them so compelling as a basis for the life of the university through the ages.

There are those who insist we must reaffirm Aristotelian reason (or more broadly, classical reason, after the manner of the followers of Leo Strauss) as the heart of the educational enterprise or lose all integrity. Their case is not without a certain merit. If we sever our ties to the likes of Plato and Aristotle, much of our teaching becomes curiously disjointed and more than a little perplexing.[24] The reason is not that Plato and Aristotle knew the truth, whole and complete, but that they did capture much of how our processes of reason naturally work to best effect.

So we have to have a place for Aristotle. But this does not mean that we need *base* liberal education on the unity of the Aristotelian system. That is to buy coherence at too high a price. It cannot conceivably do justice to all we have learned to do with the powers of mind in the intervening time, all we have supposed, denied, reformulated, looked into, and checked out.

The issue then is to find a unity behind what we now know and know how to do. The problem is to get the integrating results of Aristotelian reason without limiting ourselves to Aristotle's philosophy. We are seeking the vantage point from which we can look back on *our* particular methods and discrete fields of knowledge, and see the common identity of their construction and the common capacities of reason that enable us to appraise their merits and limitations as works of the mind.

We know now that scientific empiricism will not be good enough, for there is more to education than the transmission of reliable knowledge about the nature of the world out there. We know that the cultivation of critical reason is not enough alone, that there is more to it than simply being aware that thought is contrived by the mind. We know, and the point *is* Aristotelian, that we are going to have to reconcile knowing and acting, understanding and appraising, science and morality.

So the matter does not hinge on our answer to the epistemological question alone. It is not just a question of what we think we know about "objective reality." We are going to have to decide how to array analytical effort across the whole range of things that people do: working, playing, caring, expressing, perfecting, maintaining, transforming, discovering, creating, nurturing, protecting. Finding out "what is going on out there" is only one objective among many.

The answer is almost on the tip of our tongue but we cannot quite get it out.

CHAPTER FIVE

Efficiency: The Mystery of Teaching and Learning

Some of us are professional educators. That would seem to imply that we have a skill: that we know how to teach. Teaching is a practical activity. Thus it should be possible to analyze our practice and improve upon it. Over time, the university should become more efficient. It will be demonstrably more effective in educating people.

Of course, it does not work that way. Most of us have only the vaguest idea of what is effective and what is not. We throw something out. Some catch on and others do not. We really don't know why.

Part of the problem, again, is that we are more than a little muddled about what we are actually trying to do. R. S. Peters, a distinguished philosopher of education, offers these quite diverse definitions of the aims of education within a few pages. "Education involves the intentional transmission of what is worthwhile," he writes. Then, "education suggests the bringing about of a desirable state of mind." And again, "education implies that a man's outlook is transformed by what he knows." Peters concludes:

> It is obvious enough, therefore, why the term "aim" is used so much in the context of education. For this is a sphere in which people engage with great seriousness in activities without always being very

clear about what they are trying to achieve, and where genuine accomplishments are difficult to come by.[1]

Fair enough. It is not just our confusion about fundamental purpose that makes it so hard to perfect technique, to systematize teaching so that we can transform minds with the dependability and precision of a laser cutting metal. For the fact remains that the whole business of teaching and learning, the very process of transferring a thought from one mind to another, is one of the more elemental mysteries. We really don't know how that works at all.

Transmitting Knowledge

The problem, of course, is that we all see things from a particular point of view and for a particular purpose. I, your teacher, have assimilated everything I know in a complex web of connections, distinctions, inferences, and applications. This is what I now set out to teach you. You, the student, in order to "understand," will be frantically trying to fit these thoughts into a pattern of relations, a web of purpose and perspective, of your own. You and I, inevitably, will see the significance of a particular pearl of wisdom in a somewhat different way. What then is it that I have taught you? When do you have it right? When do you make a mistake?

The test of reliable knowledge is supposed to be intersubjectivity. We are supposed to see the advantage of looking at a phenomenon in the same way, defining it in identical terms, operationally, so that we can identify its presence or absence by what we have done. But the understanding we establish experimentally covers but a small portion of what we must know—and teach.

Do any of us use the same mental imagery to think about the Doppler effect, photosynthesis, simile, the Reformation, narcissism, Newton's First Law? (I think of Newton's First Law along lines suggested by Stephen Toulmin, as an "ideal of natural order." The idea that perfect motion is constant straight line motion is crucial in shifting from Aristotelian to Copernican astronomy, and makes gravity pivotal in explaining, for example, why ships leaving harbor do not sail off the edge of the earth.[2] I'll bet you don't think about Newton's First Law that way at all.)

So far, we are talking only about the transmission of knowledge, which must be the simplest, most straightforward task of education. The object is no more than to make an idea in my mind appear in yours—to pass it on. I tell you what pathogenesis, or judicial review, or expressionism is, and test you to see if you've got it right. But the moment one goes beyond textbook definitions, and asks how one might most effectively and accurately communicate ideas like these, the whole process begins to seem utterly unmanageable.

Consider. I am trying to teach the rudiments of Plato's doctrine of the forms. My own approach is to present this as an entailment of the way we reason. How can we say that something is "unjust" or "not so good" unless we have in mind, as referent and comparison, an idea of justice, or excellence? But she asks, "Did he mean the forms were really out there, in the world?" Well, *did* he? Is she picturing a perfect triangle plastered against the sky? Or is she seeing dimly the whole big idea that the ordering patterns we see in matter might mean *something?* How do I make sure she's got it right? How do I know *I've* got it right? Can she think of the forms "any way she wants"? How do I get her into the shared intellectual inheritance of her people but on her own terms? And how, pray tell, can I teach this so that she sees the *implications* of the idea, so that a sudden glimpse of the possibility of it all knocks her completely off her feet, the way it's supposed to?

We can teach students to "give back" precisely our perspective. But what we really want to do is to get them to assimilate new knowledge into an evolving pattern of understanding of their own. This means that they will, inevitably, understand the subject differently than I do. Yet, allegedly, we are passing on a common stock of trustworthy ideas and reliable methods. When, then, are they "seeing relations" and when are they "missing the point"?

"Catching On" and "Going On"

Of course, the aim of education can never be the mere transmission of knowledge. We pass on information merely to prepare the ground for something else—something big—to happen. That "something else" can never be taught directly. We can set the stage, intimate, proceed by indirection. But all of a sudden, the student must *see* that this isn't a story about going hunting at all: it's about looking for God. That the biology course, in moving from simpler to more complex organisms, is recapitulating the process of evolution itself. That Kant's categorical imperative can lead you to see that arbitrary inconsistency is unjust, logically, necessarily, universally, whatever else you've heard about the futility of asking the big question, "What is Justice?"

We want students to see the forest for the trees, to catch on, to see the point, the underlying principle. Whitehead thought the aim of higher education was to learn to generalize.[3] We want students to discover pattern, to see significant relationships and distinctions, to subsume particulars under general categories, to make judgments: this is an example of symbiotic relation; that is consistent with the law of dispersion of gas; academic freedom is not just the same as political freedom of speech.

The intrinsic function of the university is to distinguish the better from the worse approaches to reason, to teach the more reliable methods of thought. Hence, a principal aim of teaching is to bring students to see the *pattern* behind the great structured systems of rational inquiry. The object is that they see the operating logic of the calculus, of botanical taxonomy, of the structure of presumption in the common law, so that they can *participate* in these intellectual endeavors, use them as instruments of thought. Like Ludwig Wittgenstein's idea of learning a language game (and Wittgenstein is very much on my mind as I write this) one wants students to reach the point where they can say, "Now I can go on from here."[4] Generally, we will know when we have achieved that purpose, for the student will show the jubilation of insight.

But how in the world do we bring the students to see the pattern, efficiently, reliably, on time? And how do we know that they actually understand the pattern, that they have it right? For these are never rigid, closed systems, containing all the right answers. They are designs for making inferences. Again, quoting Wittgenstein, "They point beyond themselves."

Now I am teaching economics. I am explaining externalities. I describe these as costs or benefits that are not incorporated into contractual relations. The orthodox example is polluting a river, thereby creating costs for parties who have not agreed to bear them. The student asks, "Is a free rider taking advantage of externalities?" Now the free rider problem comes from another part of the forest. One thinks of the "free rider" as someone who doesn't join the union, assuming that if others do he can take advantage of increased wages without incurring the costs of membership. The context of the free rider problem is collective action, that of externalities, market failure. Yet the polluter generating externalities *is* like a free rider, seen from another angle.

Then the student asks, "Is foreign trade an externality?" Now I'm sure he's wrong. But he goes on to explain, "If the manufacturer moves a plant to Taiwan to escape higher domestic wages and regulations, isn't he *sort of* a free rider?" Well, what do I say now? Do I correct or commend? Each of these answers is somewhat askew. But is it not possible that the student has *caught on* to how economic reasoning works, that he has shown he can "go on from here" better than the one who sticks to the orthodox categories? Or is all of this too loose and intuitive, not a *rigorous* understanding of economic analysis?

The purpose of the university is to teach the best methods of thought and to correct students when their reasoning is not as good as it could be. But what does it mean to see the point: to understand how to go on? And what does it mean to make a mistake, or not yet have it quite right? Consider this example from Wittgenstein:

> But there is also *this* use of the word "to know"; we say "Now I know!"—and similarly "Now I can do it!" and "Now I understand!"
>
> Let us imagine the following example: A writes a series of numbers down; B watches him and tries to find a law for the sequence of numbers. If he succeeds he exclaims: "Now I can go on!"—So this capacity, this understanding, is something that makes its appearance in a moment. So let us try and see what it is that makes its appearance here.—A has written down the numbers 1, 5, 11, 19, 29; at this point B says he knows how to go on. What happened here? Various things may have happened; for example, while A was slowly putting one number after another, B was occupied with trying various algebraic formulae on the numbers which had been written down. After A had written the number 19 B tried the formula $a_n = n^2 + n - 1$; and the next number confirmed his hypothesis.
>
> Or again, B does not think of formulae. He watches A write his numbers down with a certain feeling of tension, and all sorts of vague thoughts go through his head. Finally he asks himself: "What is the series of differences?" He finds the series 4, 6, 8, 10 and says: Now I can go on.

Or he watches and says, "Yes, I know *that* series"—and continues it, just as he would have done if A had written down the series 1, 3, 5, 7, 9.—Or he says nothing at all but simply continues the series. Perhaps he had what might be called the sensation "that's easy!" (Such a sensation is, for example, that of a light quick intake of breath, as when one is slightly startled.)

But are the processes which I have described here *understanding?*[5]

I have said that the object now is that students catch on to how a system of reason works. But is there only one system? Should things add up in one particular way? I am teaching social contract theory—Hobbes, Locke, Rousseau—so that they can understand the foundations of liberal reason. But she is assimilating what I teach to a growing pattern demonstrating the pervasiveness of paternalistic domination in Western thought. He is seeing the roots of the rationalization of class relations in capitalist ideology. Are they *missing the point* of my teaching? Does their distraction mean they will not be competent to use some of the most important intellectual equipment of our public life? Should I insist that they see it my way? Or are they entitled to their "point of view" and that's the end of it? Or is there a portion of truth in each perspective and is our task now to create an acceptable synthesis? Or should I try to show why liberal rationalism is *more important* than feminist political theory or Marxism?

There is a fine line between "knowing how to go on" and "jumping to conclusions." One does not understand Hobbes if one thinks that the "lust for power after power that endeth only with death" refers to political megalomania, nor does one understand philosophical pragmatism if one thinks "working in practice" means simple expediency. We *test* whether students have understood the logic of a system of ideas by examining the inferences they draw, the subtlety of their judgments. The student who can show through a chain of reasoning how a right of privacy could have been inferred from the language of the U.S. Constitution is obviously more in command of the method of liberal reason than one who just "senses" that "it ought to be there."

The great frameworks of thought—liberal rationalism, mathematics, physical science—are essentially open systems. Their implications are never exhausted. Like chess, the number of moves inherent within them is logically indeterminate. Hence, one comes *really* to understand the possibilities of such systems only by stretching them, by testing our inferences that are risky, dubious, defiant. And then the problem of the teacher is to decide whether the inferences are appropriate or not.

Again, I am teaching Plato's doctrine of the forms. He asks, "Is it like imagining hitting a home run before you go to bat?" Well, is it or isn't it? Do I correct him or applaud him?

For such reasons, William Warren Bartley III, a disciple of Karl Popper and Friedrich Hayek, speaks of knowledge as "unfathomable." We never know the full implications, all the consequences or potential applications, of what we teach. Newton could not have anticipated Einstein, yet Einstein's discoveries were an outgrowth of Newton's principles. Darwin could not have anticipated that Spencer and Marx would try to create a social science parallel to the biological model of natural selection. The creator of a theory, the author of a book or invention, never knows what it might be used for, to what further knowledge it might lead. In this sense, we have no idea of the full meaning of the systems of thought we so gladly teach. Bartley, following Hayek's view of the implications of imperfect knowledge, draws the conclusion that inquiry must be understood as an open, self-organizing, marketlike process. At least, we never have any right to prescribe the limits of a system of reason.[6] But where does this thought take us? Is it never possible to *misuse* a system of reason?

Obviously, we don't want students to do physics or philosophy by rote. We want them to be sane, sound, and responsible, yes, but we also want them to be creative. Now creativity is an attractive ideal. It connotes freedom, carefreeness, casting off inhibitions, breaking the rules. But *within* the frame of an endeavor of reason, creativity cannot mean simple self-expression or "doing just as you please." Creativity as a *contribution* to a rational enterprise is always an achievement of discipline. It is a manifestation of power under control.

Creativity may mean developing a personal style within a classical pattern. It may mean creating an interpretation. It may mean catching on to a larger pattern. It may mean coming up with a distinctive technique. It may mean seeing things from a fresh angle, a different perspective. But novelty is creativity, not merely idiosyncracy, only when it actually is seen to expand the boundaries and possibilities of a system of activity. And this implies that it emerge out of deep understanding of a way of doing things, out of that perception of pattern that enables one to say, "Now I can go on."

Consider this. I am *still* trying to explain Plato's idea of the forms. She asks, "But wouldn't it make more sense to think of the form as what something develops into, like an acorn becoming an oak tree?" That's Aristotle, I tell her. She looks perplexed. I probe. I discover that she doesn't know a thing about Aristotle. Whether she picked up the acorn example somewhere else or not, *the strange fact is that she has essentially rediscovered Aristotle's response to Plato all by herself.* (Astonishingly, this sort of thing happens all the time. Students anticipate Locke's response to Hobbes, Mill's to Bentham. They *infer* the next step in the unfolding logic of Western thought.) Still, does all this mean that she has really "caught on"? Or is it all just an accident? Or is it a fluke of the collective unconscious? Or the *Weltgeist* acting up again? But could she have done this at all without grasping the pattern, without seeing the point, and being able to go on by herself?

Just how big a picture do we want students to be able to see? Our academic departments are all specialized subdivisions within a larger frame of reference. Law, economics, and political science are simply derivations and applications of a larger logic of liberal rationalism. Physics, biology, and chemistry are forms of scientific understanding. How does one hook up the larger vessel to the smaller one? Does one really catch on to the idea of fraud, or market efficiency, or the tension between individual right and majority rule, until one has grasped the foundation idea of contract on which these other concepts are founded? Can one catch on to the purpose of physics or chemistry unless one sees such specialized subjects in relation to the general search for the principles of order underlying the transitory and contingent flux of the world that started somewhere in the neighborhood of Miletos about three millennia ago?

In any event, I think we stand a better chance of *predictably* getting to the point where the lights go on if we relate the larger philosophy to the particular discipline, and vice versa. All of this is part of making the purpose of the endeavor clear. The specific sciences begin to make sense as part of the history of the human project of trying to grasp the meaning of the world. Conversely, the most fundamental questions of knowledge and knowing take on substance only when one can relate them to mathematical proof, scientific generalization, and literary allusion.

We can weave an infinite variety of patterns of thought depending on our dispositions, our interests, and what we have learned before. The right of the teacher to correct or commend, to *insist* that the students see the system *this way,* can rest only on some fundamental idea of purpose, of the object of inquiry. You can think of Plato's forms "just as you please," unless the aim is to understand objective idealism as a possibility of reason. You can think of the history of liberal thought as a study in paternalistic, or class, domination, but the object at the moment is to understand it on its own terms.

And the reason we so desperately want students to see the system one particular way, the *same* way, is so that they can become full participants in some unfolding project of thought. So we are back again with the idea behind the specialized organization of the contemporary university. The object is really not that students should "think for themselves." Rather, knowing is common and collaborative. For understanding to *advance,* we must think alike and we must also think differently, but above all, we must think together. The diverse imagery we employ to understand for ourselves, our varied perspectives and the implications we draw, count as *contributions* only when they are clearly pertinent to the object of the endeavor. Otherwise, they are illusion, or error, or simply beside the point.

Specialists and Generalists

But is this not an oversocialized view of the process of teaching and learning? Have we not lost sight of the individual, emphasized the Hegelian at the expense of the Lockean dimension of thought, as one might say? Certainly, the aim is not to subordinate individual thought to the system. Rather, the object, in such a theory of education, is to induct the student into a discipline, a pattern of thinking, as full participant, criticizing, judging, creating within it. The point is that the student be able to use the method *independently* as a guide to judgment, understanding, and action.[7]

Still the question naggingly remains. Is this quite enough? This is, to be sure, how one would want to prepare scientists, judges, or journalists. But shouldn't liberal education imply something more? We want, we say, people of broad vision. We have too many narrow specialists. We want people who are wise, humane, competent, people who can grasp the problem as a whole, can see the big picture. But where, may I ask, do we teach these things *directly*. Show me the syllabus please, for the basic course on wisdom!

The fact of the matter is that all we have to teach are the disciplines. If we are going to teach something greater, we are going to have to teach it *through* the disciplines. Now we come to the most baffling part of all. How, technically, can we use the teaching of the specialized and specific to bring students to grasp the general and the whole? How can competence in a particular method lead to competence *generally,* competence as a virtue, something that goes beyond method? Leaving aside the pious simplicities of commencement addresses, it is not at all clear how we can do this. Achieving transcendence as part of the daily routine is not as easy as it looks.

What in fact are we trying to do when we see the disciplines as *instruments* for the general development of the individual mind and spirit? Opinions differ, but all of this must have something to do with seeing the pattern and being able to go on. Perhaps the aim is to get students not simply to catch on, but to catch on to catching on. We want students to get on top of our system of methods. The point is that they come to see the disciplines as a kit of tools. Teaching is showing how to penetrate to the heart of the pattern, to see the purpose, to use the diverse schemes of ideas precisely, cunningly, tellingly, judiciously. We are *really* teaching not astronomy or anthropology but seeing relations and making distinctions, drawing inferences, criticizing, appraising the limits of systems, applying them in a variety of situations. Fine. But what method, which course of study, is *most likely* to elicit productive thought?

Some might want to argue that our present method, of taking students through a disconnected jumble of courses, semester after semester, accomplishes precisely this purpose. To survive, the student must be intellectually nimble, skipping quickly from topic to topic. Perhaps this is what we expect "generalists" to do, to grasp the rudiments, however superficially, of the disciplines, so that they can figure out what the scientists and economists are talking about, at least as that is portrayed in the press, so that they can make conversation when the topics of art and literature come up. We often talk this way. Liberal education is portrayed as something of a survival course, jungle training for those who would make their way in the intellectualized circles. But something here smacks of sophistry. And all of this is more apology than philosophy. Again, we are back to the notion that anything you take might be good for you, that every subject is good exercise for the mind. Again, such a position represents nothing more than an impregnable defense of the status quo.

The hard fact is, as the university is presently constituted, broad insight, if it occurs at all, comes more or less by accident rather than design. Daydreaming in lecture, one *sees* that a mathematical equation might be treated like an analogy. What appears on one side of the equals sign is *like* what appears on the other.[8] Perhaps this is the best we can do. But perhaps it is not.

What we are looking for at this point, perhaps, is some way to secure the individual element in thought. We do not want to subordinate the individual to the system. The aim of liberal education, like a liberal government, is to empower the individual. So we want the individual to get on top of the system, to grasp it whole, to make it personal.

The problem is as old as philosophy. The individual thinks. But thought is a collective product. We think only in relation to a common *body* of thought. We cannot actually think totally alone. However, there is something wrong if we think only the thoughts we have in common, if we never think for ourselves.

On this basis we can say, at least as a practical matter, that the problem of teaching is to steer a course between identifiable extremes. On the one hand, we do not want students to learn physics, or philosophy, simply by rote. On the other hand, as I have insisted throughout, we don't want students to "think for themselves" if that means "just as they please." We want students to think in relation to some discipline. We are justifiably worried about what students will do on their own. The vagaries of their own minds may lead them astray, prevent them from understanding, from catching on. Surmise can be a peril, to each of us, to all of us.

This means, as a matter of daily routine, that with split-second precision we have to say, of every effort of students to make the disciplines their own, "That's right," or "That's wrong," or "Maybe." Thus do we deal, at the nuts and bolts level, with the problem of mind in the world. This is how we nudge the *Zeitgeist* merrily on its way. And if truth were told, most of us haven't the faintest idea of how to do this. It is largely a matter of hunch and instinct. We might as well explain walking a trapeze or riding a bicycle. But our business is reflection on unexamined practice. Is it possible that we could learn to do what we actually do when we teach?

"Drawing Forth" the Powers of the Mind

Again, the aim is not to fit the individual to the disciplines but to organize the disciplines so as to develop the capabilities of the individual. And to develop the powers of the individual in a certain way, so that the individual can be contributor to the general human venture. The problem, still, is how to go about doing this.

The verb "educate" is derived, etymologically, from words that mean "draw forth" or "draw out" from some incipient or rudimentary state. Now this is provocative indeed. How does one go about "drawing forth" the powers of the mind?

The idea suggests that we are dealing with *something that is already there*. This sounds remarkably like Plato's conception of *anamnesis*, that learning is remembering, teaching reminding. The possibility is less incredible than it appears. Does it not *seem*, when one "recognizes" the pattern, that one is suddenly aware of something one has seen *before?* I have no intention of plumbing the depths of this strange thought. I bring the matter up just to show again how little we know about what is going on when we educate and how uncanny the powers are that we try to propitiate. Just where is, and what is, this mind that we try to draw forth?

Is it *strictly* an individual power that we try to draw forth? Surely this is what many of our contemporary theories of education suppose. We all have specific talents and capacities. The idea is to make the most of one's potential. Education should be tailored to the needs, and the promise, of the individual. Thus, we ask students to react to a phenomenon on their own terms, to develop a personal interpretation, to express their "feelings" about the matter at hand.

But is the aim actually to accentuate what is *different* in each of us? Is the purpose that our understandings be as *distinct* from one another as possible? I have said that, unavoidably, we are going to learn differently, see things from diverse perspectives. The issue is whether the object is that we each develop a unique point of view.

What does it mean to draw forth the powers of the mind?

She concludes, after careful study and reflection, that liberalism teaches an egoistic and relativistic morality and is therefore inadequate as a public philosophy. Is she *entitled* to this opinion? Or should she be *required* to reach a fuller understanding?

He says that he has finally understood the relation of the "Big Bang" theory of creation to the biological theory of the spontaneous development of life and he is now a deist for, on the basis of the evidence, after the first moment of time, there was nothing for a Creator to do. Has he demonstrated an adequate grasp of the subject? Or should he be asked to consider other cosmological theories and their theological implications?[9]

Perhaps the aim is that each student develop a personal philosophy. But when has the student developed a *satisfactory* philosophy? When is the task of the teacher done?

Again, is the purpose that each develop a personal way of understanding? Or is the aim to bring the student to see what we can all see, what we can understand in common? Is the mind individual? Or is it universal?

There is so much that is inevitably individual in the process of learning. It is affirming and denying. ("No matter what the professor says, I still don't think you can explain everything as capitalist hegemony.") It is being persuaded and changing your mind. ("I used to think abortion was murder. Now I see how complicated the problem is.") It is making commitments. ("I will be a biologist not a chemist. I will be an idealist not a relativist.") It is making applications, choosing the right system of reason for the problem at hand. ("I don't think it's a matter of simple economics; I think it's a question of fairness.")

Still, the aim of education is not simply to see things your own way. It is also to see things the way we all can see them. Hence, if education is drawing forth the powers of the mind, that mind is not exclusively the mind of the individual, it is mind in the grand sense, in the spirit of Plato and Aristotle, Kant and Hegel.

So, at some point, the student has to glimpse the possibility of "general understanding"—and rationality.

I am teaching the history of political thought. I am trying to bring home the Roman Stoic notion of natural law and natural justice, a law common to all people, whatever their customs or particular political traditions and institutions. So I say, "The requirement of the course is that you all will write two papers, but *you,*" I say, pointing to a student at random, "are going to write three." "Why?" he asks, in shock and outrage. "Just because I say so," I respond. This works every time. I have illustrated beyond any doubt what Edmund Cahn calls the sense of injustice.[10] We know, viscerally, instinctively, that this is unjust, long before we have reflected on the meaning of justice, long before we have formulated a principle of justice.

Drawing forth the powers of the mind may be more a matter of evoking the mind we have in common than getting everyone to express a "personal opinion." Still, we could not base a liberal education on the idea of *knowing* universal truth. There just isn't enough of that to go around. In the end, we have to get on with the business of teaching those partial, contingent, inadequate truths embodied in the disciplines. Yet recurrently, during the routine process of getting an education, one should glimpse the possibility that something big is going on here, that in some respects, astonishingly, the universe is *comprehensible* and that we all do have a fundamental sense of right and wrong. One need not dwell too long in such regions. The university is really not the place to sit all day enraptured, contemplating the eternal verities. This power is better captured in sidelong glances. As natural beauty can overwhelm us only in brief doses, and then it is best to get back to hiking, or paddling, or chopping wood, so natural law and the universality of mind is something it is best to come upon, unexpectedly, in all sorts of odd places, in the course of doing other things.

Why Education Is Wasted on the Young

Of course, we do not see the point all at once. Understanding grows gradually. Each year, each decade, the web of relations grows denser and clearer. New things, things we thought obvious or trivial before, now strike us as remarkable. In such respects, the history of the individual mind is like that of the mind we have in common.

Yet strangely, we have organized higher education on the apparent premise that the capacity for insight, for general, reflective thought, is best cultivated in a short, intense burst of time in late adolescence and early adulthood. We are bound to be disappointed. But a handful, we know, of all our students will actually grasp the pattern underlying the details of their studies. We often chalk this up to differences in intellectual ability. But much of it could be a matter of time. I am always astonished at the significance I see now which I did not see six months ago.

Twenty is not an age of mature judgment. How is one supposed to understand politics when one has not yet made an adult decision, a decision that affects others? How is one supposed to understand scientific procedure when one has not yet had time to be perplexed, and patiently and persistently *forced* a problem out into the open? How in the world is one supposed to cope—and all at once—with the psychology of existential despair, the moral significance of the Holocaust, the despoliation of the rainforests, the genetic code, subjectivity and objectivity, and this in the midst of learning to live with a roommate, decide on a lifework, endure ebullient and crushing romance, and put up with all the demeaning and humiliating experiences that come with being young and aspiring but at the very bottom of all the ladders of social organization?

Of course, it will be protested, formal education is supposed to be no more than preparation for lifelong learning. But is it sensible that the process end so abruptly? Do we really believe that at the end of four years we have set a trajectory which will lead, inevitably, to the continued unfolding of the powers of the mind? Again, the rhetoric is familiar but the whole idea that we have a plan of education well contrived to the end in question is absurd. Most remarkable is the apparent assumption that individuals, after graduation, will continue to develop intellectually in isolation one from another. How many closet readers of Plato or fundamental science do you find in darkest suburbia? The fact of the matter is that we can count on a sustained process of intellectual development only when people are engaged in work that demands it, as some parts of business, the military, government, and research indeed do. And this does lead people back to the academy from time to time. But such results are fortuitous, not systematic.

It would be well, at this point, for us to reconsider formally the cultural convention that liberal education is the culmination of schooling. Granted, the conventional mold has been broken and we now have students of all ages. But culturally, we still think of universities as places set apart, inhabited predominately by the young. I shall have more to say, as we go along, about the interweaving of the universities with the various professional callings. But perhaps the essential point is somewhat more fundamental. Perhaps there should be universities on every street corner, as there now are churches, and it would be assumed that many would attend them, as they now do churches, regularly throughout life. And the primary mission of such centers of continuing education (call them Lyceums, or Athenaeums, or even Chautauquas, if you like) would not be certification in marketable skills but perfection of the endless process of catching on, seeing the point, and being able to go on from here.

Turning Point

Learning is a matter of seeing the pattern. It is also the desire to do well, to carry out a complex work with excellence. That, indeed, is the power we want to draw forth, nurture, and perfect.

Thus, once again, the argument folds back upon itself. For it is precisely our effort to discern an underlying pattern, to catch on to what the university is all about, that is guiding this inquiry into the aims of liberal education.

Gradually, step by step, we have considered ideas that are intended to define the essential purpose of the university. As we draw out the implications of these proposals, we become aware that each in turn leads to a point where we sense that this particular conception of purpose in fact *prevents* us from going on, that it excludes, or distorts, some element that we sense should have a place in a working philosophy of education. So we have a problem of proportion and, more fundamentally, of *arrangement*. Each of these considerations has a place in the pattern, but none is sufficient to constitute the pattern itself.

By this point, we are at least able to recognize that we are using a method of thought to establish the qualities of a method of thought that might define the aims of education. Some may think this way of proceeding suspect, but I defy them to tell me precisely why it is suspect and to come up with something better. After all, one must follow *some* method in coming to conclusions about the requirements of method.

It is now time to turn from rumination to conjecture. To this point, we have been deliberating diverse perspectives, contrasting possibilities, casting widely about for ideas of what liberal education should be. Now it is time to draw the threads together. The mood of analysis changes from critique to argument. We leave the open water and move with the flow of the river. It is time to focus on a single theme, to see where it carries us, whether it can serve as proposal, guiding principle, hypothesis, and *ratio decidendum*, the point on which the decision should turn.

CHAPTER SIX

The Cultivation of Practical Reason

Now we need a plan and a program. We can no longer pretend that one assortment of courses is as good as another, that anything a student wishes to study is sufficient to provide a liberal education. We have to define the relationship of the parts to the whole. We have to show the point of what we presume to teach. We need an idea of purpose that is sharp and clear enough for us to know when we have succeeded or failed, yet broad enough to accommodate the elements we know must be there. It is no secret that I hope to find this guiding theme in the idea of practical reason.

Integration

I hope the idea of integration can help us here. The word *integration* has the sense of *making* whole, or bringing *back* together. It suggests that there once was, or potentially always has been, a completeness in the elements present. The task of integration is to draw forth a pattern that is already there. The aim, as in all practical reason, is to bring the going concern closer to its ideal image. Only revolutionary doctrines assume that you can start over anywhere you please. Integration, like any method that requires continuity, is a discipline.

In searching for an integrating theme, we start from our list of requirements and expectations, the elements we assume must be part of the pattern. We try these one at a time, asking whether any one could serve to organize the whole. We test these possibilities, each in turn, by asking whether it provides a proper place for all the other elements, or whether it excludes or distorts something of importance.

Thus I have asked: If we organize our efforts around the formation of citizens, or enculturation, what becomes of disinterested inquiry? If we take our aim to be the cultivation of scientific objectivity, do we preclude commitment and engagement? If our purpose is to transmit reliable knowledge, what becomes of the creative, the conjectural, the poetic elements in thought? I have moved step by step in this way. Now it is time for me to try the idea of integrating purpose that I think might fit.

The Nexus of Practical Reason

I have defined practical reason as the activity of examining a pattern of practice, and criticizing it, analytically, reflectively, with an eye to its improvement. Practical reason is a matter of distinguishing excellence and error. It also implies mastery, the effort to do something as well as it can be done.

The idea, of course, has Aristotelian roots, and thus recalls the spirit of systematic rationality that unified the university through many ages. But, we will recall, this was also the idea that gave integrating purpose to the American university in its formative decades. The point of systematized, organized, professionalized inquiry, again, was indeed to improve our ways of knowing, but it was also to perfect our practical ways of acting, all our crafts, and skills, and arts, and professions.

Note carefully, I am not arguing then that the American university is fundamentally corrupt. I am not suggesting that we must start all over again on new foundations. My aim is to enhance the performance of the going concern, not to condemn it. In a way, I am trying to remind us of where we seemed to be going before we lost the trail, trying to recapture the urgency of a sense of mission that we seem to have lost. But then the question becomes, of course, whether we still believe in this sense of mission.

Those who follow in the classical tradition often insist on a distinction between theoretical, practical, and technical reason.[1] I intend to collapse that distinction here. After all, the disciplines of pure theoretical inquiry (consider physics or mathematics) are organized around ideas of appropriate practice, as in any other kind of endeavor. And the purely technical fields ought to be philosophically reflective about the purposes behind their techniques. (Should not engineers persistently ask: "But what is good design, anyway?") For this reason too, the old dispute between liberal and vocational education, between learning-for-its-own-sake and learning-to-get-a-job, simply doesn't apply.[2] And again, I advocate this integrating principle not simply because it is socially useful but because I think the role of engaged participant that it encourages is more humanly desirable than that of captious critic, detached spectator, calculating egoist, or instrumental puzzle solver, which seem to be the implicit alternatives if we organized around the cultivation of any other current model of reason.

What Would a Commitment
to Practical Reason Entail?

No integrating principle is neutral. To constitute a pattern is to make a decision to see things this way rather than that. Inevitably, we will exclude certain possibilities and emphasize others. (Scientific theory is no different. To endorse Darwin's biology or evolutionary geology is to rule out certain teleological understandings of the meaning of life in the world.) The problem then is to decide willfully, aware of the commitments we thereby accept and those we will forsake.

What would it mean to accept the cultivation of practical reason as a way of defining the aims of liberal education? First, we must assume that intellectual progress is possible, that we might just be getting better, perhaps even getting closer to the truth. To some, this may seem unremarkable. But many in the world-weary contemporary university would wish to disassociate themselves from such an awkward thought. They know we are just spinning our wheels. To affirm a belief in intellectual progress is not very fashionable at the moment.

Of course, the idea of practical reason does not mean that progress is inevitable, or that the latest is the best. We may have missed the point or gone astray. In fact, the search for best practice implies a constant scanning of past practice, for what we are really after may be something we abandoned, mistakenly, at some point in distant history.

Similarly, the method of practical reason does not assume that the questions of the meaning of the world or of our conduct in it will eventually be settled. Inquiry is an unending quest. But *that* in itself is an undemonstrable assumption about knowing and the knowable. It implies that we can know something but not everything, a very strange a priori assumption when you stop to think about it, though it is the dominant epistemological proposition in our philosophic heritage.

Given that a commitment to practical reason does rest on such a "foundational" assumption, there are those who will say that this is just another theory, and there is no reason why this particular view should define the program of the university. We should teach this philosophy, like all the rest, as one opinion among many. But then, it would seem, we must ask what the entailments of basing our educational program on *that* philosophy might be.

To accept the cultivation of practical reason as the integrating principle of our educational program is also to assume that the university will not be separated from but implicated in the affairs of the world. The whole point is that every human endeavor should become more intelligent. This means the university will scrutinize, and try to improve upon, the practices of the state, business, the arts, medicine, the media, our conceptions of the proper use of arms and the proper stewardship of the earth, and all of this in close collaboration with the practitioners and professionals in these various endeavors. Some think this will inevitably corrupt the university. Others think this is exactly what a university should do. This is a forced choice. There is no way to have it both ways.

In sum, to accept the promotion of practical reason as the central educational aim of the university is to affirm that the Enlightenment project is still tenable. It is to assume that the intellectual venture of our civilization is not exhausted but, in fact, may have hardly begun. But such beliefs as these are not simply assumed in the contemporary academy. In some quarters these are fighting words. So to propose practical reason as the operating ideal of the university is not to seek an uncontentious consensus. It is to take a stand. But there is no uncontentious idea of purpose we could endorse without losing all hope of honor and integrity. The issue, as always, is simply which conception of purpose best fits our image of what a university is supposed to do.

All of that said, let us now press on to see what a program of liberal education based on the cultivation of practical reason might look like.

Sequences of Thought

There is a natural order to the teaching of practical reason. This does not mean that you can reduce practical reason to a mechanical formula, like those textbook caricatures of scientific method that read like instructions for assembling lawn furniture. ("1. Formulate a hypothesis." Or worse, in policy analysis, "1. Rank your values.") I know as well as you do that constructive thought does not work that way. (Technically, the real method of purposive thinking in every field is the same. You sit staring, turning over one thing and then another in your mind, hoping something bright will happen. It is precisely the same as prayer, or meditation, or mysticism.)

Nonetheless, there is a logical progression in teaching practical reason, for this method of mind makes sense only if it is seen as a series of skills, each of which presupposes the previous one.

I shall first lay out a schema, a conception of how practical reason might best be cultivated. Then, in the next chapter, I shall sketch an idea of the curriculum, a picture of the way the disciplines might fit together to achieve these purposes. The design is open and flexible. It invites innovation and experiment. It is intended to set the stage for public deliberation on the future of the university. In the last chapter, I shall ask how that deliberation might best be conducted.

Mastery

The aim of education is to teach best practice, the most reliable methods of thought. The first task of the teacher then is to explain the practice, and to show why it is presumed best. Thus, one presents the method and defends it at the same time.

The corollary is that the student, ideally, should try to learn to do something as well as it can be done. We call that mastery.

This means that education begins in assertion, not in doubt. We do not start by showing the confusions and uncertainties of the field. We do not begin with criticism. We do not teach the argument. We lay out the foundations in bold, declarative strokes. We conceal the fact that we could have chosen another starting point, gone about this in a different way.

The student knows too that in the first stages trust is required, not skepticism. The teacher who is too concerned to present all the qualifications that scholarly meticulousness requires is greeted with restlessness. Get on with it! I need to see the main point!

This initial stage of instruction does not last long. Soon one wants to see what can be done by varying the elements, trying things out. Diligence is replaced by curiosity and experimentation. You start to do this as soon as you can see the pattern.[3]

There are natural stages in learning to do anything, from home repair to metaphysics. First you learn to do the thing at all. Then you do it yourself. Finally, you do it your own way. (First you find the notes and play a simple tune. Then you imitate your teacher. Then you try a piece on your own. Finally you interpret. You can't reverse the order.)

I have said the *initial* aim is mastery. Can this possibly be right? Isn't mastery the *culmination* of learning? To be sure, you can think of mastery as a process of continuing tutelage that ends only when you can play the most difficult pieces or execute the most demanding research projects. But this is not a very efficient method of education, and it is not the approach of practical reason. Here the aim is that students learn to correct and perfect their own performance. The object is that they learn *how* to master something. And the key to this conception of mastery is that students learn to compare their performance with some underlying ideal of purpose, some fundamental critical standards, almost from the start. This tells us virtually everything we need to know about how the teaching of practical reason must begin.

How do we get our students to see this ideal of purpose, this strange presence which enables us to criticize, improve, and perfect, but which we can barely discern ourselves? There are basically two approaches. We can present exemplars. Or we can *justify* our teachings.

To teach students the arts of mastery we often present examples of outstanding work. We have them read *Moby Dick,* listen to Sibelius, study *The Federalist* as an example of political argument at its finest. Sometimes we say that our aim is only that students should learn to appreciate fine writing or fine art. But again, is our intent only to cultivate a consumer's perspective?

Still, we must inquire. What do we have in mind when we present exemplars? Do we really expect our students to write like Melville—or Madison? Of course not. This would create a certain recipe for frustration and failure. Still, we do not encourage them to write like pulp novelists or to think like hack politicians. The only thing we can conceivably be trying to do through this process is to invoke an ideal standard, a ground they can use to appraise their own performance—and that of others.

We might let these exemplars speak for themselves, hoping students will recognize the qualities they represent. Or, through critical analysis, we may try to spell them out. We may try to make explicit the standards inherent in the enterprise. Of course, we can also do this directly.

The second approach to teaching the self-criticism that leads to the potential for mastery is to present best practice and its rationale at the same time. In other words, we try to justify our teachings. This kills several birds with the same stone. First, we give a public account of the grounds on which we presume to teach the right way to think, an act, as we have noted, that does seem to require justification in a liberal society. In doing this, we must make clear the essential point of the discipline, and the standards we have employed to distinguish best practice from its alternatives, what should be taught from what should not. And all of this, of course, provides a framework of ideals and norms that students may use to appraise and correct their own performance.

There are two basic ways to justify a prescription for thinking: the systematic and the historical. Either one shows how the parts go together, functionally, organically, to constitute a whole, or one rehearses the process of inquiry by which present practice came to be regarded as best practice. In either case, note, the teacher is *protagonist* of orthodoxy. It is not yet time to display all the dirty linen, to confess all the confusion and controversy that surrounds the teaching. First one must master the discipline and use it. First you do things according to the rules. Then you learn how to break the rules in the interest of doing something even better.

To be sure, the teacher may want to present alternative perspectives, but the reason for justifying a practice is to show why the *official* perspective is to be regarded as preferable. Systematic justification means that we try to show why one idea of method should be expected to work better than any other in achieving the objective at hand. It means showing the attributes of this design for a machine, or a building, or a government, or a science that are presumed to make it superior—thus making manifest the grounds on which we might appraise *any* machine, or building, or government, or science, as excellent or wanting. The object is that the student see not only the ideal but the *worth* of the ideal.

The alternative is to show how practice developed historically out of a process of deliberate, evolutionary effort ro resolve the puzzles and paradoxes, the limitations, of earlier usages and understandings.

Thus, one does not simply launch into the study of orthodox neoclassical free market economics. Rather, one reviews the increasingly static fabric of guild and manorial productive institutions in medieval Europe, the development of state regulatory mercantilism in France, Prussia, then in England, as a kind of nationalizing of the guild system. Then one takes up the Industrial Revolution, the release of entrepreneurial energy and productive power precisely in those areas of north England and Scotland where mercantilism had been least enforced. Then one teaches Adam Smith's theorization—and defense—of the emerging system as the ground of liberal political economy.[4] Now you are ready for the basic textbook treatment of the theory.

Or, instead of plunging directly into classical mechanics, as is standard practice in virtually all introductory physics instruction, one reviews the gradual evolution of a cosmology based on Ptolemaic astronomy reconciled to Aristotelian physics. One recounts the growing paradoxes and anomalies of the system, the complex efforts to account for the data yet save the theory. One speaks of equants and epicycles. Then one describes Copernicus' Pythagorean confidence that nature must be simple, his gradual awakening to the heliocentric view, the subsequent efforts of Kepler, Galileo, Newton, to complete the picture and provide a physics, and a philosophy, adequate to the new order of the cosmos.[5] Then, perhaps, one is ready to teach physics.

To teach the point of practice historically does not mean we have to suggest inevitable progress. Rightly done, the story of any tradition of inquiry will be a very human tale, filled with fundamental error, blind groping, stubborn intransigence, gross stupidity, and improvised, clumsy solutions. It is not only the success of Copernicus, Kepler, and Newton, but the extraordinary wrongness of the basic cosmological and physical assumptions that guided inquiry from ancient times through the Middle Ages that is startling about this story. The message is not just that science succeeds. It is also that we could be fundamentally mistaken again; in fact, we are probably quite wrong about something we think is certain. (Fundamental doctrine in geology, biology, and political theory has been revised in my lifetime. Where will the next fundamental truth be transformed into fundamental error?)

To see the quest for good practice in its grandest, most dramatic forms may be the quickest, surest route to teaching mastery. Still, the controlling objective is simply that students learn to criticize and correct their performance according to the characteristic standards of the field. Whatever method we choose, this is the criterion by which we must test the success of our pedagogy.

How do we know when our students have caught on to this capacity for self-correction that I am calling mastery? What precisely does it look like when we succeed?

She is about to write the sentence "Since I was raised a Catholic, I cannot endorse abortion as a simple matter of individual prerogative," and suddenly realizes that a motive is not a reason, and an explanation is not a justification.

He is designing a research project and now sees clearly why, without a control group, his results will be meaningless.

She is trying to argue that Aristotle is fundamentally democratic, given his view that we are by nature political animals, and now is trying to figure out how to reconcile that with his clear statement that in an ideal polity only the virtuous would be citizens. In the end, she reverses her thesis.

He has been reading about the Argentine wheat boom, the Brazilian coffee boom, the Venezuelan oil boom, earlier in this century and now realizes that third world countries have not necessarily always been grindingly poor, and he begins to rework his thoughts about the world economy around the peculiar problems of raw materials exporters.

Is any of this so extraordinary or exceptional? Is this not, in fact, precisely what we would want our students to be able to do as a result of *any* program of liberal education?

The first aim of a system of liberal education that would cultivate practical reason is that students learn to correct their own performance according to a discipline. To be sure, this is a capacity to be perfected through a lifetime. But is it not perfectly realistic to think we can instill the durable habits of mind pertinent to this end in the ordinary course of a liberal education?

Critical Reason

I have argued that criticism should not be the principal aim of liberal education. The cultivation of critical reason for its own sake can only lead to cynicism or to an unpleasant mood of fastidious connoisseurship. But if criticism is seen as an aspect of the teaching of practical reason, the matter appears in quite a different light.

To criticize is to assess the merits of a work or effort. It is necessarily a deliberation of excellence and imperfection. By its nature, it requires that one invoke standards and ideals. There are really, I think, four distinct levels of critical reason that we will want our students to pass through, each one taking us closer to that reflexive inquiry into purpose which is the heart of practical reason.

First we learn to criticize and correct our performance according to the rules of good practice, the ideals and examples we have learned in the process of seeking mastery.

However, in the second stage—and this is where critical reason properly begins—we learn to take the measure of the performance of others. We are taught to appraise a work of art according to canonical norms, public policy according to liberal principles, scientific statements according to accepted ideas of appropriate method. We learn a certain discernment. This character in the play seemed wooden. This pattern of taxation might have unintended consequences which would be inequitable. Global warming might be caused by increased fossil fuel consumption and then again it might not. There are too many factors in the historical record and the data remain ambiguous. At this stage of learning practical reason, we begin to criticize, but we criticize according to received doctrine, according to the acknowledged rules.

At a third level, we learn to criticize not a particular performance but the terms of reference of a practice, a general way of doing things. We attempt to size up not only the merits of this particular painting but the general state of contemporary art. Not only do we ask whether this political procedure is democratic but we inquire also into the merits of democracy as a form of government. Not only do we criticize just this scientific investigation but we ask also about the state of the field of study of which it is a part. The issue is not only whether this finding is valid, but whether the paradigm of research has been drawn too tightly, whether the presuppositions of the discipline itself are credible. At this point, we begin to appraise not only the performance of others but the standards of the practice itself.

At this point, we begin to wonder about standards and methods, about accepted ideas of what is worthy and what is not. We take exception to the official views, to the criteria of good performance we have been taught. We pass beyond mastery. We begin to do it our own way. We consciously test the limits of the acceptable in art. We begin to ask probing questions, fundamental questions, about the tenability of the public philosophy. We perhaps imagine questions, and approaches to inquiry, that are closed to orthodox science. And at this point, a greater wisdom begins when we recognize that orthodoxy is not always wrong, that discipline is more often enabling than constraining.

Finally, then, if all goes well, we enter a fourth stage of critical reason. We become self-conscious and learn to take the measure of our own thought. What, we ask, makes us so cocksure we have it right, we who are so ready to defy convention? Are we really prepared to assert, in full responsibility, that the enterprise would proceed better if others followed our lead and renounced settled opinion? Out of such doubts, and commitments, we undertake critical deliberation with ourselves. If we are resolute, and lucky, we may begin to forge a philosophy.

Now in the passage from criticism as self-correction to criticism as the appraisal of performance and practice, something else that is quite remarkable has happened. For we now realize that this broader exercise of critical reason is in fact a public act. It is an aspect of *political* participation, of citizenship, in the most ancient and honorable sense of the terms.

We are taught conventionally that citizenship has to do with voting, running for office, and the like. But to deliberate on the performance of an industry, a science, a profession, or a government is in fact to engage in the public debate. Once we appreciate the implications of this, we cannot help but see not only education but the political order itself in an entirely new way.

In classic liberal political theory, a sharp line is drawn between the public and private realms. Public life concerns only the affairs of state. All other human enterprises and activities are supposed to be private affairs, of concern only to those who are parties to them. Thus, we speak of private enterprise, the separation of church and state, the autonomy of the university. But if we take the public character of critical reason seriously, we can't stop there. Now we recognize that there is a public interest in the performance of the industries and professions, the crafts and trades, the arts and sciences. Three chapters ago we saw how this public interest becomes manifest in defining the purposes of the university. It is the same with any other purposive enterprise.

None of this implies that the state should regulate all purposive activity. Nor does it mean that all organized practices should be responsive, democratically, to the will of the people. We need a much more subtle political theory than that to handle what we have just discovered about the nature of practical reason. We have to begin to think of the polity not simply as a relationship between individuals and government, as is conventional in liberal democratic theory, but as a complex relationship between government, individuals, and the intricate pluralist regime of purposive enterprises, which are in essence self-governing, but also, since they perform a public function, in some way responsive to the people as a whole. And we have to begin to think of political deliberation as a dialectic between the practitioners and the public concerning the way in which these vital public functions are properly performed. This leads us finally to understand that our efforts to criticize and to improve the performance of our *own* craft or profession are a form of political activity, perhaps far more vital to our role as citizens than those more peripheral activities of voting, going to meetings, and the like that we normally associate with citizenship. And once this is said, we realize that a practice or profession *is* a form of government, and that like a democratic state, it must be open to continuing deliberation internally on its success and failure. In fact, this becomes a crucial test of the *legitimacy* of a corporation, a profession, or a discipline in a society which comes to realize the close connection between the basic tenets of liberal democracy and those of practical reason.[6]

Thus we see that an education designed for the formation of citizens and one designed to develop practical reason are one and the same thing. And while I have stressed the public nature of critical reason in this discussion, we should realize that this criticism of the performance of one's profession is also crucial to the perfection of one's personal skill, to mastery.

To engage in critical analysis may be essential to learning how to do something "your own way." The medical student has come to be acutely aware of the limitations of advanced medical technology and resolves that in his own practice he will be cautious about overprescribing its use. And I know, very intimately, one political scientist who thought in graduate school that he would learn theories and techniques that he could apply to solving public problems. He found the theory and technique he was taught not particularly helpful, and decided he would have to make some all by himself.

The Arts of Judgment

Education begins with assurance. One teaches the discipline, the reliable foundation knowledge, the prescribed methods of thought. Mastery, at least initially, means learning to do something the right way, according to the rules. Criticism begins by evaluating a performance against accepted standards. But at some point, this straightforward approach, in any subject, must yield to a more complex vision. We must show the student that it is possible to think otherwise about the matter at hand. We must, often with some regret and a slight sense of betrayal, undermine the students' confidence in the soundness of what they have been taught.

This relativizing experience is an essential part of liberal education. We introduce it in many different ways. Sometimes, we teach historic error, stressing how often established opinion was dead wrong. Sometimes we teach the way people of different cultures, ideology, or religion might understand a matter differently than we do. We go to lengths to point out that even our sense for the soundness of mathematics might be different if we came from a culture that thought in terms of one, two, and many. Or how our intuitive sense for objective reality might be different if we had twenty-nine words for snow. Or we teach the argument, we show how scientific findings can yield ambiguous truths, how it might be possible that the earth is warming, and then again, maybe it is not (that the world might end in fire, and then again, perhaps in ice). Or we attempt to show how our most cherished institutions might look from the point of view of the oppressed. Thus do we bounce the minds entrusted to our care around, insisting on the straight and narrow path at one moment, at another requiring them to become totally bewildered, unsure about even the fundamentals of their understanding of the world.

Why do we do this? Why do we want to shake them up in this way, spin them around, so they can't tell up from down, inside from out? What is our purpose in trying to dispel certainty and instill doubt, especially when we do it, as we often do, with such relish and glee? For some, doubt is essential to independent thought, but we have already examined the complexities that position, in its simple form, leads to. And we have seen that as a partisan undertaking others wish to disabuse students of belief in the power of reason itself.

But the effort to introduce perplexity and bewilderment into the curriculum has a very specific and clear purpose when the overall aim is to *enhance* the capacity for practical reason.

If our aim is the improvement of practice, we must at some point find prevailing practice inadequate. And a way of thinking becomes inadequate—puzzling, problematic—precisely at that moment when it can't account for something it should.

If our methods of thought are to improve, they must be confronted with inconvenient facts. So raising neglected perspectives, pointing out anomaly, is a crucial part of the work of systematic, rational inquiry. Those who teach reliable knowledge have a strong interest in keeping it that way and hence a disposition to pretend not to see phenomena that clearly belong to the domain but do not fit the theory. It is simply part of good practice, loyal service to the discipline, to insistently point this out. But, as we all know, this is dangerous work. Those who pursue it are often officially described as traitors, heretics, cranks, and crackpots.

Still, raising inconvenient facts and neglected perspectives is really part of critical reason. And it cannot be an end in itself. The next stage is deciding what to do about the awkward situation. This calls for a different temper of mind, a different quality of thought, which I call the recognition of problematics and the exercise of adjudicatory reason.

The reliability of a method of thought is tested by its generality, by its capacity to fit unanticipated conditions. A belief, or a theory, works well in practice if it can be applied to—if it "covers"— a wide range of experience. We face puzzlement and perplexity only when a rule does *not* help us, when our beliefs, or our customary ways of doing things, do *not* work out in practice. We are stymied. At a loss. We cannot "go on from here." And that, as Peirce suggested, is really where inquiry begins.

What we are really looking for at this point is a better theory, one that assimilates the new situation to the existing framework. The more inclusive theory is the better one. This is, however, an act of creative reason, and an ideal solution to the problem. For we may not be able to solve the problem in a way that satisfies the community of inquiry, the body of qualified, disinterested observers. "Eureka!" is usually a solitary shout. It is seldom proclaimed in a chorus.

Still, simple inclusiveness is not the aim of inquiry. The fundamental work of the university is still to distinguish the better course of reason, and to separate truth from error or illusion. Hence, when rival theories or perspectives confront one another, the essential problem is not to find a way to make them all fit, but to figure out which to use as a guide to action. This process occurs all the time in the deliberations of the university, but it is perhaps better illustrated by the law.

The problem of the judge in the common law tradition is, in essence, to decide what to do when a principle of settled law is seen to be capable of being interpreted differently, seen in new perspective. And it is the assumption of the common law that the law *grows* by discovering how established principles can best be adapted to fit fresh situations.

There are basically three decisions we can make when we face a problem of adjudicatory reason. We can *deny* that the mooted new interpretation requires any adjustment in established doctrine. We can *show why* it seems unreasonable, or we can distinguish the point at issue from the principle invoked. (Abortion is *not really* an exercise of the right to privacy. It does not concern the woman and her doctor alone.) Or we can attempt to *integrate* or *reconcile* the new position with established law. (If the fetus is not regarded as a person in the eyes of the law, then the abortion decision is as private as any other decision that affects only the agent, and there is no state interest in its regulation beyond the safety of the procedure.) The third possibility is to *accept* the previously neglected perspective, showing why previous doctrine was in error. (In *Plessy v. Ferguson* separate but equal public facilities were construed as meeting the requirements of equal protection of the laws in the meaning of the fourteenth amendment, but with the evidence adduced in *Brown v. Board of Education* we now conclude that such facilities are inherently unequal.)

In law, in science and the arts, in any profession that has a conception of best practice, we make these decisions all the time, and each creates a new pattern of doctrine for the enterprise. The life of the mind is, in the end, less about inspiration and discovery, and more about reasoned decision, in situations where no answer is unambiguous. In any human endeavor, these are momentous decisions. They should be faced with fear and trembling. And in the process of liberal education, we should teach our students how best to confront them.

In any field, there is no other way to teach adjudicational reasoning than to confront students with dilemmas and predicaments, with diverse theories and perspectives, and ask them which should prevail, and why.

It is not enough to teach students simply to appreciate the viewpoints of others. Tolerance is an important quality, we wish to develop it, but in practical reason, the process cannot end there. For once we realize that it is possible to act, or appraise, or think, in different ways, we shall have to decide *how* we shall act, or appraise or think, and which modes of acting, appraising, and thinking we shall encourage others to adopt. We shall have to ask which of the ways is better. Again, we sense the public nature of practical reason. We do not actually decide these things for ourselves alone.

Creativity and Innovation

Creativity does not mean simply doing something differently. It means doing it better. Creativity emerges out of perplexity. It is when established paths are blocked (or we are not sure where they lead) that we search for a new way.

Thus, to teach creativity is first of all to teach puzzle and paradox, the things that go awry, that don't work right. The object of teaching criticism, and the problematics of diverse perspectives, is to stimulate creativity, the quest for resolution. Adjudicatory reason is tragic choice, it is a way of proceeding in the face of a dilemma. But the aim of creative intellect is actually to *resolve* the problem at hand, to come up with an identifiably better approach.

Sometimes creativity takes the form of *demonstration*. This is what we do in ordinary science. It is a matter of finding a way of *showing* that one possibility is better than another in reaching toward the end of action. It is to show statistically that early childhood influences may be more important than formal education in overcoming poverty and prejudice. It is showing that it is better to think of light as a particle than as a wave in these circumstances.

Sometimes creativity means *integration,* seeing pattern where none was evident before. Sometimes it means *extending* a theory, a method, a style into new terrain, pushing the form of the novel, or the formal model, to represent things we did not think it could represent before.

Sometimes creativity means *distinguishing,* showing an essential difference between things we lumped together so that we can, in fact, discern the whole more acutely—as Aristotle did in distinguishing essence from accident.

Sometimes creativity means *depicting* something better than has been done before. We reduce diversity of perspective by finding a better perspective. And isn't this always a matter of coming closer to the essential idea of purpose, still vague and inchoate, but always before us?

Mastery means doing something well according to the rules. Criticism means appraising a performance or practice according to a system of standards linked to inherent purpose. Is it not clear that these are stages in the development of thought that are prerequisite to creative effort?

Creativity always seems an act of defiance. It is always done *against* those who insist we must follow the rules (this is the limitation of sheer mastery) and those who insist that it can't or shouldn't be done (this is the limitation of sheer criticism). However, creativity is a form less of rebellion than of collaboration. Creativity, after all, is not resistance to discipline, but an effort to perfect it. It is, however it may appear, a form of participation, not merely individual expression.

And this means, of course, that the sequences in the development of practical reason run in both directions. It is the master, dissatisfied, who becomes critic. It is the critic, inspired, who becomes creative. But, in reverse, it is the critic who must judge the worth of the innovation. And it is the master who must discover how well it performs. (The design of the unorthodox airframe emerged out of careful scrutiny of previous designs. It has been subjected to rigorous analysis in every detail, on the drawing board, on the computer, in the wind tunnel. Now it is up to the test pilot to fly it, try it in every configuration, to find the *limits* of the design.)

The aim of practical reason is the improvement of practice. Creativity is the aspect of thought which leads to the proposal of better ways of doing things. This means that a program of education which would cultivate practical reason must *aim at* creative effort as its culminating objective.

Now creativity is a will-o'-the-wisp. It can occur, as we all know, anywhere, anytime, to anyone, and it can frustratingly elude those who most desperately need it and are best qualified to find it. Yet everything we do as educators is so extraordinary anyway, why should we not also try to make the conditions for the emergence of creativity as predictable, routine, and reliable as possible? I have argued that a program that leads from mastery, to criticism, to problematics is most likely to accomplish this objective. This, then, sets a standard for the appraisal of the curriculum and our teaching. Are we willing to say then that those who teach but mastery, or criticism, or problematics, and who disparage the possibility of doing better, are not worthy of their calling?

Transcendence

The purpose of liberal education is to bring students *fully* into participation in the life of the mind. This means that at some point, when they are ready, we have to take them into the high country and give them a glimpse of the land that lies beyond the mountains. At some point, we have to raise the largest questions: What does it all mean? What is in fact going on here? And who are we, the ones who ask such questions and try to find out?

In practical reason, such questions arise naturally, inevitably. It is simply a matter of following the method, relentlessly, all the way to the end.

As I have said, the principle of corrigibility is at the very heart of the idea of practical reason. The fundamental aim of inquiry is the critical examination of usages, techniques, methods, to see if they can be improved, better suited to the purpose they are intended to serve. Now it logically follows that since practical reason is itself an idea of practice, of appropriate method, it too should be subject to critical scrutiny, corrected and perfected, in light of some underlying idea of essential purpose. We may reach for the stars then, simply by turning the method on itself.

I have never said that the idea of practical reason was the culmination of the adventure of the mind. I have merely argued that this is a way of pulling together an idea of the mission of the contemporary university that seems most consistent with our considered expectations for what it should do. But this is the same as saying that this seems to be as far as the powers of mind can reach for the moment. And that begs the question: where do we go from here?

Let us consider the situation of thought in our century. We live in a most unusual period in the unfolding of the mind. The contemporary university was born at a time of great confidence in the power of inquiry. We were certain of the progressive nature of science and the beneficial effects of its handmaiden, technology. We assumed that the cultivation of disciplined inquiry in all areas of human endeavor would be both socially useful and personally liberating.

Now we are not so sure. Our science has become less straightforward. Our physics and biology hardly ratify the clear, commonsensical views of Newton, Harvey, or Pasteur. Rather, they open onto a world of great strangeness. We have become skeptical of the powers of both technology and technique to improve our lot or heal our wounds. Philosophically, we have acquired the habit of deeply questioning the power of reason itself.

Viewed against the total saga of the development of thought in our civilization, the life of the mind in our era is curious and disconcerting. We continue to press on, with steadfast persistence, with apparent zeal, confidence, concealing our doubts, if we have them. We continue to research, and to teach, precisely as though we knew what we were doing. In the sciences, particularly, the rhetoric is the same as ever. We are constantly pushing back the boundless frontiers of knowledge. We are wonderful. In the classrooms, we lead our little bands of campers through the dark woods, whistling cheerily, not letting on for a minute that we are no longer certain we are on the right trail.

We have broken the bounds of our method and we have not found the way to put the pieces back together again. The harmonious natural laws of Enlightenment physics, politics, and philosophy no longer circumscribe our world, and we have not found a way to restore coherence.

We are perhaps still too close to the *facts* we have discovered for proper perspective. We are still reeling from the almost simultaneous acceptance of the geological account of the age of the earth and the modern cosmological account of the size of the universe. The sound, sober, scientific evidence about the immensities of space and the antiquity of existence, not to mention all the upstart things we have learned about the intimate details of the life process, has not made the universe more comprehensible, but more mysterious. We are more in awe, not less so, for all our disciplined understanding. Those of us who *know* what is going on now see the world more as did the primitive mind we thought we had displaced, in dumb wonder, not at all with the easy familiarity of the Enlightenment philosophers.

We can no longer properly account for either mind or matter. In the name of science, to make science work, we accepted a materialist metaphysic and ethic. We said that to be scientific, we had to drive explanation back to raw material cause. But we cannot make this stick. The immensities of geologic and evolutionary time made the materialist account of nature plausible. *Anything* could have happened way back there. We could weave totally new myths of creation when so much was lost in the mists of such a distant past. But all of this made the *presence* of mind in the universe a good deal more mysterious. The *fact* of thought in the universe, our ability to discern order, cannot quite be suppressed, but when the significance of this fact dawns on us, *particularly* against the background of the official materialist account of creation and evolution, it only makes things weirder. Neither "the starry universe above" nor "the moral law within" gives comfort anymore. They are astonishing, disturbing, discomforting, confusing.

We live at an odd moment in the life of the mind, but we do not know what time it is. Is the date 1490 or 1575? Is it just before the Copernican Revolution or just after? Are we playing out the last hands in a system like that of late Scholasticism, one grown much too complex and cumbersome, just before someone comes and something happens and things become "clear" again? Or are we still dumfounded by all that we have just learned, and now we must have time to reflect, slowly, carefully, to create philosophy, to see a new pattern, so that we can once again go on as did those who had to reassemble thought and meaning in the wake of Copernicus?

Whichever is the case, we owe it to our students to be very candid about all this. We have to explain it fully, on the large scale. We have to tell them how uncertain we are. We have to tell them how wonderfully dumfounded we have become.

It is simply inherent in the method of practical reason that we keep trying to wrest more meaning from an appallingly reluctant universe. Thus, in confronting the problematics of fundamental thought in our times, our puzzles and predicaments, the quite practical aim is to see if we can contrive creativity—if we can steer someone to invent something new. We want to be able to peer over the rim, to see a little further, to do a little more, a little better. Of course this is a labor of Sisyphus. We know that perfectly well. Of course those who presume a tragic sense of life will look on us gravely, as they always do, as the irrepressibly innocent children of light. We never thought they would think otherwise.

We know perfectly well we are not going to know everything. However, we also assume that it is possible to know more than we do now. These things are a matter of faith—and defiance.

I have said that the purpose of the university, through all the ages, was to find out what could be done with the powers of the mind. I have also said that the heart of any system of practical reason is the examination of present practice, to see if we can do better. Thus, in a program of liberal education founded on the cultivation of these habits of mind, ultimate questions *will* arise, routinely, automatically, as a matter of course. For simply to be clear about our purposes, and thus to appraise our performance, to ask whether we have taught people to think well or poorly, *we will eventually have to ask what mind is supposed to be doing in the world*. At this point, all barriers and pretensions crumble, and science and religion have to meet.

A Short Diatribe on the Separation of Science and Religion

One of the strangest features of the organization of thought in our times is the intentional, institutionalized separation of science from religion. Through all the ages, it was simply assumed that inquiry was linked to worship, that human reason reflects, if dimly, divine reason. Science and philosophy were always regarded as sacred vocations. This was simply assumed at Athens, at Alexandria, throughout the Middle Ages, and by most of the great thinkers of the high Enlightenment. Our era is startlingly different in this regard.

Today, it is widely assumed that science and religion are not only distinct but antagonistic. Throughout this century, scientists and philosophers have often taken their task to be to disabuse students of the superstitions and myths propagated by organized religion. The churches, particularly the more conservative ones, have increasingly seen it as a central mission to proclaim the faith against the overpowering forces of secularism, represented particularly by the universities and the public schools.

In fact, this by now ritualized combat between two equally crude and ignorant battalions does not do justice to the diverse and subtle theological speculations that have accompanied scientific inquiry at the higher reaches of the thought of our times. It is not so much that our greatest thinkers have thought science and religion incompatible, as that in our time they have been less sure of what to make of the connection. Einstein simply believed that the design of God was manifest in the simplicity of natural law. Charles Sanders Peirce thought that there was one interpretation of a phenomenon that was "fated" to be agreed to by all observers, and he saw this capacity of mind as a proof of the existence of God.[7] Wittgenstein first sought a truly unambiguous language, in which words mean the same for everyone. But in such a language, he realized, we could never speak about the most important things. These would be shrouded in mystery.[8] (Later, Wittgenstein opened his *Philosophical Investigations* with a long discussion of Saint Augustine, who, of course, insisted that knowledge of God would not come through human effort, that only divine illumination would make things clear.) Max Planck took the more conventional view that science and religion pertain to separate but equally valid realms, the first to material reality, the second to morals and values. But Teilhard de Chardin discerned in the organization of evolution, and the presence of mind in the world, a scheme that has the effect, perhaps, of confirming Christian revelation. And the fathers of quantum physics, including Werner Heisenberg and Niels Bohr, often associated with the "relativizing" of science, brooded deeply on the larger implications of their ideas. In the end, they came to think that *understanding* could only mean grasping the principles of "the central order," that knowing ultimate reality could only be like knowing the soul of another human being.[9] The thought of our epoch is anything but uniform, and our best thinkers have often suspected more than they, in their scientific scrupulousness, were willing to avow in their theory.

The practical problem that we must face, and decide, of course, is how we should teach the relation of science and religion in the university. It will do no good to simply insist that the university has no business dealing in religion, or, in public universities, to appeal to the separation of church and state. No one is suggesting that we teach denominational doctrine. Like it or not, we are implicated in the business of finding meaning in the universe, and teaching students about the proper place of humanity therein. In deciding what should and should not be taught about such matters, it makes no sense at all to exclude some alternatives simply on the ground that they involve "religion."

How should we go about deliberating this question? Let me suggest that we begin, as artlessly as possible, by asking directly what it is that we think a religion is supposed to do.

Essentially, I suppose, a religion is a system of practices designed to bring people into closer communion with God. In our culture, we expect it to be a dense condensation of all that is meaningful. We expect it to combine a metaphysics, an aesthetics, and an ethics, reduced to a vital core that, with powerful impact, transmits a vivid image of the presence of God in the world and a straightforward conception of right and wrong. We want the message to be well suited to the needs of ordinary people, and to the instruction of the young. Our practical sense is that the churches are not only houses of worship. They also have a civic and a moral role to play. They are supposed to teach the difference between good and evil.

The difficulty, of course, is that this system of instruction runs parallel to that which is dedicated to the critical analysis of practice and tradition, and while the teachings of the secular system steadily increase in their level of sophistication, the instruction offered by the religious institutions most often remains at the same basic plateau. Thus, as one grows up, the worldview of the university often seems to supersede that of the churches and, in the end, one "puts aside childish things." (Obviously, if scientific education stopped at age twelve and one went on to study advanced theology, the result would be precisely the reverse.) But the greatest difficulty is that, today, in our culture, these two systems of education proceed in almost total isolation one from the other.

Again, the aim of practical reason is to examine prevailing practice to the end of its improvement, so that it better serves essential purpose. Yet it would seem unlikely that the protagonists of orthodox religion would accept the idea that the practice of religion could be improved by systematic analysis. Nor is it likely that many in the university would think it their proper work to criticize religious practices so that we might design methods of worship that would bring people closer to God. Yet in every age and culture (this is no Western idiosyncrasy) but our own, this has been central to the mission of philosophy, science, and the university. Among the many odd results of this separation of faith and reason unique to our times is that while we tend to think of science as a progressive enterprise, we regard religion as a finished product, a tradition to be preserved, but not perfected.

There is no way to go back. It would be totally beside the point to try to restore the medieval university or the denominational colleges of the nineteenth century. That is all now in the past. But how in the world shall we learn "how to go on from here"? It is a real problem, a matter of deep perplexity. But this might also be the next step in the evolution of the powers of the mind.

In any event, when we reach this very brink of our capacity to understand, it is certainly right to teach the problematics and not doctrine. We have no reliable knowledge to offer. This is surely where we want to display the diverse perspectives, the differing ruminations, of those who have come as close as they could to life and the universe in our age, and wondered. Perhaps a few who study now will wonder too, and they might just see an opening. And perhaps we will build an entirely different approach to education on that foundation a hundred years from now.

CHAPTER SEVEN

The Core of the Curriculum

All we have to teach are the disciplines. If we are going to improve the educational performance of the university, we must work with the materials at hand. We wish to broaden minds but we cannot wait for a faculty composed only of those of great soul and broad vision, or a curriculum based entirely on timeless, illuminating truths. We will have to make do with what we have: ordinarily competent academic specialists teaching flawed doctrines. The trick, then, is to pull the pieces together so that the whole represents somewhat more than the sum of the parts. Philosophy and organization must substitute for inherent scarcities of raw talent and trustworthy technique.

To proceed in this way seems consistent with the longer idea of the American university. But where once the object was to contrive a system in which normally capable minds could produce new knowledge, reliably and predictably, now the aim is also to fashion a program that will educate people to think creatively and constructively, as a matter of routine.

Let me review, once more, the essential elements of the problem. First, we need to specify a relationship among the disciplines which will satisfy both our public expectations for the university and its intrinsic capabilities, what it can teach with integrity. Then we must find a place for the diverse fundamental commitments that impel, even as they divide, the academy today. There must be a role for those who would preserve cherished tradition and those who would promote self-conscious skepticism of all conventions of thought. There must be room for those who seek knowledge for its own sake, according to rigid empiricist or philosophic norms, and those who pursue the kind of rough but durable wisdom that can be useful in guiding action to desired results. Finally, we must see how the scheme leads efficiently toward the unfolding and maturing of the powers of practical reason, as that was outlined in the preceding chapter.

Now, ideally, I suppose, each and every discipline should be constituted as a perfect community of inquiry, complete and whole, and ought to convey in its curriculum all the elements essential to the exercise of practical reason: mastery, criticism, confrontation with problems and puzzlement, judgment, creativity, and that final, culminating sense of awareness of what it means to be alive and thinking in the world. Of course we could use this model for a critique of teaching in any field, pointing out that some subjects are taught so that students are frozen at the initial level of mastery, some fields are notoriously incurious about their own presuppositions and epistemology, and so on. But again, the key point is that any discipline can be thought of ideally as a vehicle for developing all the dispositions of mind that are essential to practical reason.

However, our project opens up a broader opportunity. Each of the disciplines, and each of the great branches of knowledge—science, social inquiry, literature and the arts, philosophy—has its own concerns, its distinctive history, and a specific, customary place in the program of the contemporary university. Each then has a particular contribution to make to the cultivation of practical reason. So the next step is to show how the major fields of study, as they are presently taught, might be orchestrated, integrated, in a coordinated plan to enhance the powers of purposive thought.

At this point, then, I am trying to see what can be done with the materials at hand. I want to take the disciplines as they are, with all the quirks and peculiarities they have developed as they sought to become learned "professions" in this century. I want to see if something constructive can come from their very weaknesses and frailties, their manifest incompleteness as scholarly endeavors. Rather than spinning out an ideal vision, I want to see if we can get something more out of the existing materials, if by stirring things up, rearranging the parts, we might find a new opening, hit on some new possibilities.

To be sure, even the most modest effort to specify a working relationship among the disciplines will seem to some hopelessly naive and optimistic. Years ago, C. P. Snow spoke of the "two cultures" of the university—the sciences and the humanities—that coexisted in mutual incomprehension.[1] Since that time, matters have probably gotten somewhat worse. Anyone familiar with the contemporary university knows that it is not simply indifference and ignorance that divide the disciplines, but far too often suspicion, derision, and contempt as well.

To Alasdair MacIntyre, the epistemological cleavages between the "encyclopedists" (or scientific rationalists), the "genealogists" (or postmodern critical theorists), and the defenders of the tradition (in this case, Thomism) are so severe that the only solution may be to define universities as the locus of competition among these warring positions, or establish different universities endorsing rival positions, and let them vie for adherents.[2]

I am mindful that even the modest program of educational collaboration I shall propose would require striking changes in established parochialisms and enmities. Yet I am unwilling to give up the battle to the extremists. Despite all the talk, it seems to me that most go about their business in the university rather quietly, largely oblivious to the battles of the rival epistemologies. Perhaps this is a blessing in disguise, a beneficent side-effect of insular, narrow specialization. In any event, my aim is to find a broad middle path down which many might travel. I have never expected advocates of any of the polar positions to agree with me.

What I shall propose is a schema for thinking about how the various disciplines might contribute to the common aim of developing practical reason. This is then a conception of the core of the liberal education curriculum, the elements that might be common to any undergraduate program. While each of the elements can be associated with particular disciplines, each also suggests a theme for collaboration among the disciplines, for projects that cut across the curriculum. All in all, it is a minimalist program, a way of taking the next step, not the last step, in our efforts to organize efficiently so as to bring forth the powers of the mind.

The schema can be read as a structure of courses but, again, I would like to leave the specifics a little vague. I would rather speak of undertakings, or projects, than a new packaging of basic requirements. I think there might be many different ways of organizing academic programs around such an idea, and I think a lot of experimentation is in order, to find out what works and what does not. Thus, I speak of the core of the curriculum, not a core curriculum.

Civilization

The aim of teaching "civilization" in this scheme of liberal education would not be enculturation. That is far too pretentious and contentious a goal. Thus we can drop the modifier "Western" from the title. This is not induction into the way of life of a people. That would be an immense undertaking, presumably ranging from philosophy to family relations, religion to technology. There must be some principle of selection, and any interpretation of such a tradition would be inherently arguable. To be sure, there are those who think the university should perpetuate a specific civic myth. But as I suggested before, the university would have to be intellectually satisfied with the myth it was perpetuating, and under present circumstances, there is little agreement on how the myth, or which myth, could be taught with integrity.

Rather, in my view, the proper function of teaching civilization is to orient students to the education they are about to receive. It is a necessary prelude to the whole process of higher education. The purpose is to teach students how we came to think as we do. Its aim is to show the genesis, the development, and the rationale of the systems of analysis, the disciplines of mind, that the university deems worthy of teaching.

Indeed, this itself is a daunting project. But here, established practice seems plausible as a point of departure. Conventionally, such courses begin with the precursors of Plato and Aristotle, pass through Roman thought, the Judaic and Christian traditions, medieval civilization, en route to the Renaissance, Reformation, and the scientific revolution. This sets the stage for the rise of scientific rationalism, the liberal democratic nation-state, along with related currents in the arts, and literature. There is room for discussion of those movements in thought and culture that have taken exception to the rise of modernism, rationalism, and the Enlightenment spirit: for conservatism, romanticism; for the study of Marx, Nietzsche and Freud.

There are many variations on such a theme, to be sure, but an underlying pattern seems generally apparent. The aim is that students catch up with the argument, to show them where they are entering the deliberations of the mind. It is an effort to show them how the structure and process of education came to be as they are. As I indicated earlier, to learn the rationale of prevailing practice is essential to mastery, to the first phases of cultivating the skills of critical, and thus practical, reason.

As I suggested earlier, to correct one's own performance, or to appraise general practice, one has to sense discrepancy between current accomplishment and an ideal aim. In teaching science, then, it is worthy that we go back to Heraclitus, Pythagoras, Aristotle, and show how their search for *logos,* for underlying order, informed Copernicus, Newton, Einstein. We may then, as we wish, go on to teach more current, positivistic notions of science in the ordinary curriculum. But the stage has been set, the longer continuities established, a standard evoked for the appraisal of current practice.

In like fashion, in preparing for political education, it is important that we go back to the sources, to show why public judgment is unlike personal judgment, why impartiality and generality matter in the realm of law. That implies reading Aristotle, Kant, Locke, and others, en route to any appraisal of contemporary affairs.

The historical approach of such a course is essential to put things in perspective. Right from the beginning, intimations of skepticism, the cultivation of a certain intellectual distance, are evident. We thought differently before, in ancient Israel or China, in the Age of Faith, perhaps we shall think differently again. There are many who have taken strenuous exception to our dominant, official views today. Those who teach such a course are, in effect, charged with offsetting the doctrinal immediacy, and in many cases, the doctrinal certainties, of the disciplines. The aim of this part of the undertaking is to begin the relativizing experience that is part of liberal education, and essential to the cultivation of practical reason.

Now the teaching of civilization historically should be distinguished from the teaching of history. It is one thing to try to reconstruct the rationale for an enterprise and quite another to try to represent the past as adequately as possible. To be sure, the historian can contribute to our understanding of the evolution of ideas and the arts, by placing them in the context of a time. However, the teaching of civilization is not the specialized province of the professional historian. The task of history is different. It is properly concerned with the totality of human society, not simply its intellectual and aesthetic ventures. The place of the historian is with the social sciences; the aim the representation of human experience.

The civilization course cannot be the exclusive province of any discipline. Properly, it belongs to the faculty as a whole. The effort is to provide, as best we can, a codified understanding of how we came to think as we do. Its fundamental mission is to present, publicly and candidly, the warrants for, and the limitations of, what the university presumes to teach. And for this reason, it is proper that such a course focus on what is often contemptuously called "high culture."

How does all this bear on the question of whether to teach the great books of the "Western" tradition or to insist that students appreciate the diversity of worldviews, within their society, within knowledge itself? Obviously, if the aim is to put the teachings of the university in perspective, it is pertinent to show that there may be things in heaven and earth undreamed of in our philosophy. Thus, it may make sense to dwell on the fact that the Mayans thought differently about mathematics, the Ashanti about law, and we might even presume to teach our embarrassingly sentimentalized version of the Native American environmental ethic. However, I would introduce one caution. The enthusiasts for multicultural education today seem intent on teaching only the *differences* in perspective among peoples. I would insist that equal attention be given to the remarkable uniformities in understanding and appraisal between cultures. Chinese philosophy, for example, can be construed as based on assumptions not so very different from our own.[3] The more I learn of the world—and I think I know several distinct cultures at the level of the soul—the more I am impressed by human commonalities, the less by exotic differences.

As I say, I would be perfectly happy to drop the word "Western" from the title of the course on "Civilization." The fact that science, philosophic rationalism, and liberal democratic political theory arose in what might very loosely be called the West is purely incidental. These are universal properties of the human spirit, artifacts of thought that are available to all peoples. I think we should be mindful of the diverse sources of this thought—their Middle Eastern, African, and Asian origins, their Latin American expressions, and I think we should be aware of the potential contributions of peoples of diverse backgrounds to the further elaboration and growth of this inheritance. But I also think we should be very careful to distinguish systems of thought that have these universal qualities from those that are by their character strictly local, parochial, the property necessarily of specific tribes and nations.

The problem in the end is to find an economizing principle. For everything we add to the conventional content of such courses, we will have to take something out. Advocates of an expanded canon seldom heed the economist's warning that there is no such thing as a free lunch. Is a week on Confucius worth dropping a week on Saint Augustine? If we squeeze in Mary Wollstonecraft to accommodate claims for gender balance, are we going to truncate our consideration of John Stuart Mill? There is, after all, already great diversity in the conventional teachings. Aristotle, Cervantes, Galileo, Shakespeare, Voltaire, Kant, and Nietzsche hardly add up to a uniform point of view. We have to be very clear about what we intend to accomplish when we add something new. The criterion against which to measure the inclusion or exclusion of any text seems clear enough: How does it contribute to the students' ability to apprehend the full intent of the fundamental endeavors of thought and spirit that frame the structured disciplines that the university has declared worthy of teaching, as prescriptive for the cultivation of our uniquely human powers, those powers that enable us, individually and collectively, to improve performance, to pursue excellence.

Science

Science is but one mode of systematic thought, one way of trying to wrest meaning from the world, one technique in the effort to make good on an idea of purpose. Yet it is scientific rationalism in a dozen guises and interpretations that gave impetus to the American university as we know it, that defined its agenda and gave, at least, a surface coherence to its efforts. In the formative years, each of the disciplines "professionalized" around some self-assumed idea of science, some norms of appropriate procedure, some rules of rigorous method.

If a basic aim of liberal education is to bring students into the life of the mind of their time and place, to equip them to participate as fully as possible in the ways of systematic thought of their particular epoch, then mastery of the fundamentals of scientific inquiry and the scientific outlook must be a prime objective of the curriculum. In a sense, science education is properly the first elaboration on the study of civilization. The historic study of the development of systematic thought culminates naturally in the emergence of the scientific worldview; now it is time to come to terms fully with what that mode of understanding entails.

Today, the primacy of scientific reason is contested. This is a time of critique and reconsideration, particularly of the narrower, unreflective versions of positivist orthodoxy. Often the target is not scientific inquiry properly understood, in the broad sense, the grand sense, the sense that links the likes of Einstein to Heraclitus, but the unreflective, routinized, bureaucratized science that seems entrenched in many parts of the university.

In any event, for students to understand what this argument is all about, for them to be prepared to engage in the critical questions of knowledge which may very well be among the more intriguing and crucial concerns of the age, they must understand what the scientific outlook entails, and this in its grandest and broadest vision, at its best.

Scientific education is also a crucial foundation for practical reason, as I have described it. Science at its best represents that ideal of reflexive, corrigible thought, of a discipline of mind that aims, precisely, at the improvement of practice. Science is more than a representation of reality. The conventions of scientific thought also are at the heart of much of our morality, and our rules of deliberate public action. As Loraine Code points out, there is a moral dimension to *knowing*.[4] Humans depend on knowledge. The community of inquiry relies on trust. Truth telling then is an epistemic responsibility. This implies a clear judgment on what we know and what we do not know that closely parallels the fundamentals of scientific understanding. Skepticism and intellectual humility are moral as well as scientific attitudes. And, as Code suggests, epistemic responsibility suggests a kind of realism, that there is a world out there to tell the truth about. Pure subjectivism would be epistemically irresponsible, though epistemic responsibility requires a keen awareness of the part subjective perception plays in knowing.

Now all of this said, we come face to face with the immediate practical problem of how to teach science in the liberal arts curriculum.

There is obviously something very much the matter with science education in the American university. The proportion of students majoring in science, or preparing for science careers, declines steadily. Worse yet, an alarming number lose an initial enthusiasm for science in the course of university education. For our purposes, however, the crucial concern is that science has almost ceased to be part of the general, liberal education of Americans. Few students venture beyond a scattering of unrelated required courses, grudgingly taken. The cleavage between C. P. Snow's two cultures seems more complete than ever, and at the level of undergraduate education it is the scientific culture that is verging on extinction.

What is going wrong? The scientists, with alarming uniformity, blame the students. They shun scientific rigor in favor of softer subjects. But this explanation is a little too self-serving. There is also something the matter with science education. Talented students, even colleagues from other fields who have taken basic courses to refresh their knowledge, report that such courses are dull, taught without inspiration or sense of purpose. Too often, a theoretical framework, a sense of overview is missing. What is stressed is fragmentary, routinized, mechanical problem solving.[5] I have asked numerous scientists what could be done to remedy the situation, and with only a handful of inspiring exceptions I have met with little but appalling indifference and incomprehension. A remarkable number seem to take their teaching task in introductory courses to be simply that of weeding out those unprepared for advanced study in science. As for improvement, few could think beyond rather jejune tricks to make science more "relevant."

What then should be the aims of science education within the general liberal arts curriculum?

Again, practical reason begins in mastery. First we learn to do things according to the established norms, our best idea of how the powers of mind are properly engaged in inquiry and action. And the closest approximations of this in the repertoire of the contemporary university certainly must start from the attitudes of scientific exploration and the norms of scientific procedure. It is the scientific disposition, in the broadest sense, the wary faith that if we check it out, make sure, take pains, take nothing for granted, then we might do better, might get it right, that is in fact the tough spiritual foundation of practical reason in the strongest sense, in the sense that has served as the main path of the enterprise of mind since the Enlightenment.

The basic task, in my view, is to teach the scientific representation of the world, of where we are and who we are, and how we arrived at this understanding. To teach this scientific world picture, in all its majesty and mystery, moving, perhaps, from the intimate details of the structure of life we have so recently learned, to the largest vision of the order of the cosmos and the tale of its emergence and development, would seem a formidable undertaking. However, in principle, it seems no more daunting than telling the tale of the unfolding of civilization itself. And well done, this would be a rocking, shaking experience, and one which might put to rest many doubts. It might show how science can ennoble, that it need neither constrict nor diminish the spirit. With any sensitivity at all, one could teach the convergence of the scientific and the religious impulse. And equally important, of course, is to teach that moral and mental discipline we so blithely call "scientific method."

Let me go out on a limb and propose, concretely, how one might go about doing this. Science has to be taught in an integrated manner. Physics, chemistry, biology do not exist in isolated compartments. All scientists know this. Thus our current practice of teaching these fields in isolation, worse, letting students dabble in two or three of them and calling this a scientific education, illustrates nothing more than our lack of seriousness about this business.

Were I to plan an efficient two-year core course in science for liberal arts students, I would begin with the culminating vision and work backward to the foundations essential to comprehend it. First, then, I would ask the microbiologists, the evolutionary and total systems biologists, geologists, archeologists, and other earth scientists, and finally, the astronomers and cosmologists, to present the most dramatic version they could devise of the current scientific representation of reality—together, of course, with their doubts, hunches, muddles, and uncertainties.

Then this group would consult with the "foundation scientists" and determine what background in fundamental physics, chemistry, and mathematics was essential to understand how this world-picture was derived. The historians and philosophers of science would then determine how the appreciation of the larger workings of the scientific imagination that underlies this whole story could best be taught. This done, we would reassemble the parts in reverse order, starting from the history of science, passing through the foundations, culminating with the integrated world picture.

There are, no doubt many other approaches that would work as well, perhaps better. But the need to restore vitality to science education is about as urgent a concern as I can suggest. For today the capacity to understand this incredible achievement of mind is being lost to our common intellectual inheritance, by neglect, by contempt. Today, for more students than one imagines, the very *content* of liberal education is a sustained exercise in derision for all that scientific rationalism stands for. But those in the academy today who so easily disparage the way of science seldom have any idea of the magnitude of the human power they so casually taunt. It is a desperate imperative that we restore scientific vision to the common life of the educated person. And note that this has absolutely nothing to do with increasing the supply of technical gadgets, or restoring competitiveness in international trade.

The Human Situation

Today, officially, if also doubtfully, we invest a rather jumbled collection of disciplines, the social sciences, with the task of coming up with some plausible response to the ancient question: "What is humanity that you should be mindful of it?" It is a great peculiarity of our age—who knows what will be thought of it a century or two from now—that it is thought that this is a question for scientific investigation, that we ought to try, in effect, rigorously, systematically, to make ourselves an object of our own analysis.

The question of whether humanity is properly studied through positivist scientific method remains contentious and problematic within the university and without, and it is worthwhile that students be apprised of the basic lines of this controversy—its history, the pros and cons, the philosophic issues involved—in the course of a liberal education. This is, however, a matter that I would include within the ambit of science education as I have described it above. In the cultivation of practical reason itself I have a different role in mind for the social sciences, one that I think makes the best use of what they have learned and created, of what they actually have to teach.

Still, I must recognize forthrightly that the very idea of practical reason as integrating theme for the process of liberal education runs counter to the spirit of the more orthodox social sciences. Practical reason takes collaborative inquiry to be the crucial and characteristic human capacity. The power of mind is the fundamental datum. Now all the established social sciences try, somehow, to understand mind in relation to something else: the unconscious, the economic imperatives of the species, hedonic calculation, institutional constraint, tradition, culture. All social science is in a certain sense reductionistic. The division of labor of the social sciences is fundamentally based on what is taken to be the primum mobile, the essential springs of human action. The pivotal question then is what is to be reduced to what, and from a certain point of view then, practical reason is simply another entry in the array of approaches to social inquiry, another effort to distill the essence of humanity. It is the one that happens to focus on mind, on self-conscious, purposive, corrigible thought.

However, if we take practical reason to be not just another "approach" to social research but the very aim of liberal education, then the standard social sciences have a particular, if somewhat peculiar, part to play. This is a controversial conception of their place in the curriculum and it is certainly not the one they would assign themselves. But this is the role that takes advantage of both their fraility and their unusual accomplishments. It is, as I say, a way of making the most of the materials at hand, of fashioning them to fit our particular purposes.

When one comes to examine the social science curriculum, seriously and thoughtfully, one is struck by the fragmentation of the picture of humanity taught by the disciplines. This is in part the result of the division of labor within the social sciences. The psychological, sociological, economic, political, anthropological, and historical perspectives do not add up to a composite, a whole, nor can any be accorded legitimate primacy, whatever the not disinterested claims of the rival practitioners. But also, and this is entirely to their credit, the social sciences have sought out *uncommon* knowledge about humanity. They have sought out those as distant as possible from our own understanding. They have looked for cultures, for folkways, for codes of values radically different from our own. They have tried to comprehend the world of the insane. With cool detachment, often courage, they have tried to grasp the state of mind of the wretched, the powerful, those who commit mass murder, those who plot revolution, those who design strategies of thermonuclear war.

The social sciences have much to teach about the diversity of the human experience. They have tried to understand humanity in its extremities. Theoretically, they should also be able to teach us about the universality of human experience, about the things we can all know, all sense, all understand. But here they generally fail us. The general laws (which, to the positivists, it is their prime responsibility to produce) turn out too often to be curiously banal and trivial. People pursue self-interest. They take their values from peers. We still have to look back to the older philosophies, to Aristotle, to the Roman lawyers, to Locke, to be struck by the deeper possibilities of the ways in which humanity might conceivably be one.

Beyond their representation of humanity, the student needs to understand the mixture of the pure and the practical that has for so long marked—and justified—the endeavors of the social sciences. Granted, there are still those who think the mission of the social sciences is to produce pure, lawlike statements. But the more persistent, and more widespread, spirit has been that understanding might lead to the alleviation of ills, even the improvement of our prospects. Thus, psychology and sociology generally see their aims as, in the end, therapeutic. Economics and political science often think of themselves as engineering disciplines, their task to be the design of institutions—the market, checks and balances, democratic forums—that would lead people, taken as they are, to seek the public good more or less in spite of themselves.

There is a lingering suspicion of the whole idea of social science in the academy, as in society at large. And frankly, there are fairly obvious reasons to question the plausibility of the effort to formulate general predictive laws about the behavior of creatures whose most distinctive trait is the ability to examine such laws and decide to do otherwise. Furthermore, liberal democratic societies have a rightful suspicion of those who presume to social engineering, or social therapy.

Nonetheless, in fairness, I think it must be admitted that our society has become a little more humane in a number of large ways, and in a myriad of details, because of inquiries and teachings of the social sciences which work to systematize compassion, to make human concern less sentimental, more effective. We are a little more efficient at counseling and consolation, we are a bit more regardful of the claims of mutual respect, solace, support, and sympathy in companies, hospitals, schools, and courts of law, when we are told that this is a matter not only of religious or human commitment but simply of best practice, of appropriate technique, for which evidence can be adduced.

In the core of the curriculum, in the initial stages of the cultivation of practical reason, I think the social sciences, as presently constituted, are fated to play a particular role. By virtue of their fragmented account of the human situation, and their focus on problematics, they bring the student face to face with a vision of reality that is perplexing, disturbing, and transparently unfinished. Automatically, they raise the questions "How in fact should I understand this?" and "What is to be done?"

The vision offered by the social sciences is unsettling and incomplete. It does not resolve nicely, as do some of the teachings of the sciences and of the arts. This gives the social sciences, and the affiliated humanities, a particular role to play in the core of the curriculum. This is the place to concentrate on producing that relativizing experience which is so essential to critical and practical reason, to liberal education full-blown. Let us then not contend with the radical skepticisms of the age straight out, but assign them their proper place in the cultivation of useful thought. This is the place to teach that organized inquiry is contingent, that each subject may understand the object distinctly, that culture and tradition impel us to construe life and its meanings in highly divergent ways. Let us speak plainly of the irrational and the perverse, the confounding and the confused, the myriad foul-ups, the betrayals, the simple blockheadedness that we must encounter, and with which we must cope.

I am not suggesting here that those who actually profess the social sciences generally share the relativizing mission of postmodernism, or deconstructionism, or radical cultural relativism. Far from it. Most social scientists are epistemologically quite uncurious, and, as a consequence, many verge on dogmatism and some, in fact, achieve it. It is not the doctrine of the individual disciplines but the cumulative effect of their teachings that creates the overall impression of fragmented understanding, and may serve to instill a suspicion of the authority of organized systems of reason.

The social sciences can raise the question of diverse perspective, but they have limited capacity to resolve it. I have suggested, to be brought to suspect prevailing practice, to see the possibility that things can be understood quite differently, necessarily raises two questions: How shall we then represent the nature of the case? How shall we then proceed? The methical, experimental approaches of the social sciences can narrow the range of possibilities somewhat. They can show that some representations of the situation are highly unlikely. They can show that some proposals for action would probably end in consequences we would want to avoid. But empirical inquiry cannot actually settle such matters. For that, only the rough, stern advice of political and moral philosophy will do. I will come to this in due course. But the time is not yet ripe. The relativizing experience must settle in. The wound must fester for a while.

The Humanities

All the disciplines created in the strict spirit of scientific rationalism are committed to teaching a sparse theory of the truth. Their aim is to teach reliable knowledge and dependable practice, the dicta that still seem to hold after they have been probed and questioned from every angle. The object of rigorous analysis, thus understood, is to *rule out* most of our ideas. These do not meet the test—or they cannot be put to the test. They cannot then be counted as warranted knowledge. They belong to the realm of dream, supposition, speculation, instead.

It is not just our science that has this quality of sparse knowledge. It is apparent in the public philosophy we teach as well. Classic liberalism, the liberalism of Locke, Smith, and presumably Madison and Mill, is said to be neutral among contending ideas of human purpose. It teaches what John Rawls called a "thin theory of the good."[6] Individuals must be free to fashion their own life plans. The state has no authority to decide the aims of life, the better ways of living. Fundamental rights, the basic processes of contract, democracy, and the market follow. Like science, liberal political theory would restrict itself to those assertions on which, presumably, we all could rationally concur. And as I noted earlier, an education based solely on such a sparse theory of reliable knowledge would be flat and unsatisfying. We suspect, and rightly so, that much more can be said about the world, and about human ends and endeavors, than can emerge from the processes of rigorous, skeptical scrutiny. If we adopted the strict rules of scientific and liberal skepticism concerning what was teachable, we would rule out most philosophy, most literature, most edifying discourse, most of our *thoughts* about the world, most of our *recommendations* about how to live in it.

Fortunately, the university has known better than to exclude all such "unreliable" knowledge from its domain. It teaches all kinds of conjecture, allusion, myth, and fable. Such teachings have not been banished from the scientific university. In fact, it might seem to be the specialized domain of the humanities to teach—and teach us how to create—such "uncertifiable" ideas, ideas which cannot be tested along positivist lines, ideas which cannot be shown to hold up in the face of rigorous logical examination.

So the task of the humanities in liberal education, I will now propose, is to teach us how to go beyond the thin theory of knowledge, to teach us how to extract a fuller measure of meaning from the world, and to provide us with deeper, more explicit, guidance on how to make our way in it. Here, Annie Dillard puts it exactly right:

> As symbol, or as the structuring of symbols, art can render intelligible—or at least visible, at least discussible—those wilderness regions which philosophy has abandoned and those hazardous terrains where science's tools do not fit. I mean the rim of knowledge where language falters; and I mean all those areas of human experience, feeling, and thought about which we care so much and know so little; the meaning of all that we see before us, of our love for each other, and the forms of freedom in time, and power, and destiny, and all whereof we imagine: grace, perfection, beauty, and the passage of all materials to thoughts and of all ideas to forms.[7]

Practical reason depends, in the first instance, on such imaginative, essentially artistic, supposings, as does science. The first thing you do when you face a novel situation is to create an interpretation of it, to *suppose* what it means, what it must be like. The art of "guessing well" must be fundamental to any problem-solving activity, from medicine to statecraft. And "guessing well" would seem to be exactly what lies behind a successful work of literature, or piece of art; it is supposing a meaning that you can't at all demonstrate is there.

It is, of course, this way in science. Science, as Karl Popper taught, moves in a rhythm of conjectures and refutations.[8] Science *starts,* not in skepticism, but in free surmise. Science then proceeds by testing acutely personal visions of how reality might be, some of them, initially, quite wild. It is too bad that we so strictly separate the teaching of literature and scientific theory, for the two have much in common; at root, they are essentially the same thing. The scientists produce a picture, an image of the world, long before they try to demonstrate that this picture fits the facts. Heisenberg considered quantum physics "a striking illustration of the fact that we can fully understand a conception though we can only speak of it in images and parables."[9]

It is interesting that neither in orthodox science nor in the practical disciplines is the art of conjecture taught as a matter of systematic routine. That task, perforce, falls to the humanities, or to the humanistically inclined in the more rigidly constituted fields.

The basic way to teach the method of personal vision is through creative writing (other art forms may complement, but they cannot substitute for, the power we cultivate by writing). The work of the writer is not just to make up stories, but to find meaning in things, and it is precisely the kind of meaning that eludes scientific categories, the kind that requires allusion, metaphor, symbol, that the writer seeks. The job of the writer, ideally, is to find meanings that we hardly suspect at all, to go to that point of intuition and feeling where we can barely discern that something might be there. Ordinary, matter-of-fact language cannot help us here, so the writer must use all the arts of evocation to communicate what it was like, to tell us where he or she has been. It is precisely the same in science, or in any of the practical arts, stretched to their extremity.

The writer starts with an inkling, a possibility. But the task of the writer is not just to make things up. The quest of the writer is not just for a unique personal vision, something only he or she can see. The insane do that. The writer is trying to communicate. And to this end, the writer must correct, and perfect, the original image in the light of a meaning that is actually out there, one that, potentially, we all can see. The task is exactly the same as in science, or any activity of practical reason. It is simply pursued by other means. And all of this implies that the writer does not write alone, but as party to an organized, ongoing, collaborative undertaking, a discipline. And the success of the writer will be judged by the meaning the writer captures, and this in relation to the nature and aims of the enterprise to which the writer is party.

We write for one another. We try to pass meaning along. And as readers, we try to receive meaning from others. This, of course, is where critical reason again enters the picture. We interpret a text, we try to discern the meaning it has for us. And then we *evaluate* the text, we ask whether what it has to say is important to us, and, in effect, to everyone else. Criticism, again, is a public act. And, again, meaning and significance are contingent on purpose. A text has a different meaning if the aim is to understand human extremity so as to prescribe therapy or reform, if the aim is religious conversion, if the aim is to teach people to scale mountains, if the aim is to sell hats.

In the context of the university, of course, the function of criticism is to distinguish the texts that are worth teaching from those that are not. This becomes the work of the professional critic.

What writings then should we teach to exemplify this human power? Which should we exclude? Today, some teachers of literature think their task no different from that of the social sciences. The text should *represent* the way of life of a people. It is like a statistic, a field report. The social scientist is apt to be a little suspicious of all of this. Granted, literature can bring the way of life of a people alive; it has great utility in teaching. But the choice of a text to represent a social reality in this way requires a discipline that the literary critic may not understand, or employ too casually. James Baldwin may or may not capture what is in the soul of African America. Günter Grass may or may not give us a useful picture of contemporary Germany. Gabriel Garcia Marquez may or may not help us to understand Colombia. The professional critics posing as cultural interpreters might have a hard time persuading even a reasonably sympathetic panel of historians, political scientists, and anthropologists that they knew what they were doing, that they had workable criteria for deciding which texts to select and which to omit.

More commonly, the task of the critic is taken to be that of ascertaining the meaning of a text. Now, again, the writer uses symbol, allegory, and allusion to try to capture aspects of reality that elude scientific proposition. The work of the critic is to "make sense" of what the writer has said, to see if meaning can be found in it, which is to say, a general meaning, a meaning we might all be able to see. The critic's task then is quality control. A text must have meaning if it is to be worth teaching. It must contribute to understanding. Else it is just a nice story. Or it is an artistic failure, an attempt to represent that cannot reach other minds.

So the work of criticism is to *certify* that a work contributes to knowledge. And in that sense, criticism's function is precisely like that of scientific scrutiny and experiment. And like science, such search for reasonable meaning can reveal only the sparse meaning of a text, that which can be reduced to more or less commonplace terms. It cannot do justice to the subtlest intimations. It cannot plumb the depths. That is up to a meeting of minds between a particular author and a particular reader.

The writer is trying to take us to the brink, beyond the readily ascertainable, and thus beyond the capabilities of science. But there is much room for charlatanism here. There are poseurs, imitators, frauds. The task of the critic is to distinguish the real article from the counterfeits. And faking it is remarkably easy.

So the canon is taken as a minimum set of works that can be certified as having an important measure of meaning, as representing the power of mind to find significance in things, and in experience. Ideally, we would teach this in precisely the same spirit that we would teach science. This is the way the world, and the human venture, seem to us now, at its best, and this is how we came to construe it in this way. This is as far as we have come so far in figuring out what it is all about.

The final task of the humanities, in my ideal curriculum, would be to teach us to instill a performance with beauty. This is not trimming, mere adornment; it is intrinsic to good practice. Form is always intimately related to function. We want "elegant" solutions to mathematical problems. We want public decisions to be equitable, which is to say, in some sense, productive of "harmony" among the considerations essential to the case. Watching a master of technique in any field is like listening to music. Even maintenance is fundamentally an aesthetic matter. Most things will run pretty well in dilapidated condition. To make them bright and shiny, to tune them to perfect running order, is basically an imperative of the soul.

How shall we teach this dimension of practical reason? Basically, our method has not been recalculated since Plato. We present students with works that exemplify beauty—music, poetry, architecture—and we hope that something will rub off. In a sense, we assign this part of the process of liberal education to academic specialists, to the professional humanists. But the customary technique does raise questions of efficiency: Will an appreciation of Bach pay off in more graceful schoolteaching? Can an appreciation of expressionist painting lead to more decorous hotel management? This is a serious matter if our ultimate aim is to enhance performance in every field of practical endeavor. Perhaps we should pay more attention to the aesthetic dimension of every discipline. I, for one, will not be satisfied until I hear that the engineers and the agronomists and the psychologists and political scientists are having high-level conferences on the teaching of beauty. This is much too serious a business to be left to the specialists alone.

The humanities, then, contribute to the cultivation of practical reason in crucial but often unappreciated ways, ways the professionals themselves seldom really comprehend. Learning to write is not merely learning to "communicate." Writing, properly understood, is the effort to grasp the more subtle, elusive meanings in the world about us, in our experiences and activities. Criticism is the effort to ascertain whether the meaning the writer finds is one that is general, one that can be shared. All of this is akin to scientific exploration, but, in its way, it goes beyond science, into those ambivalent and murky regions where so much of our lives are lived, where so many of our most responsible judgments must be made.

Practical Studies

The aim of liberal education, as I have defined it, is to teach those general habits of mind which will pay off in good performance when applied to any constructive endeavor. Yet while it seems profound, and a bit bedazzling, to focus on these fundamental powers of thought, the overall effect, in case you had not noticed, is somewhat lofty. I'm not sure that the argument so far will be totally convincing to those who start from the proposition that it's a tough, hard world out there, and the object of education is to learn how to make a living. Just how this ideal of liberal education is really pertinent to the affairs of the world has not yet been demonstrated to the satisfaction of the always skeptical students whose hearts and minds we hope to win. To listen to a doctor talk through a complex diagnosis, or to hear a manager discuss a difficult business decision, is to see the relation of theory to practice, to have the dispositions of thought we have been so assiduously cultivating come alive in the world.

For this reason, I think the core of the curriculum should include the study of a few versions of systematic practice in some detail. What I have in mind is a series of courses in which various professions would describe their own conceptions of best practice, and the history of the process by which that conception of appropriate technique was developed. I imagine quite an array of electives, ranging from architecture, civil engineering, forestry, nursing, through journalism, light construction, counseling, factory layout, food processing, insurance, or the disciplines of arms. In such courses, professors and practitioners might discuss, philosophically and reflectively, what they do and why they do things that way. Nothing quite like this presently exists, for the applied fields have been concerned primarily with the education of practitioners. They have not thought of themselves as part of the general process of liberal education.

It will take imagination to develop such courses, and I realize that many of the initial efforts will be awkward at best. Philosophical reflection is not a prominent trait of many applied professionals. Here I can only hope that the invisible hand of the academic marketplace, the strong incentives that will exist to attract the best students to such courses, and, potentially, to the professions in question, will stimulate the development of courses that will illustrate the general principles of practical reason that it is the task of the core curriculum to nurture. And who knows, the very exercise of creating such courses might stimulate some self-conscious reflection within the applied disciplines. It might actually improve their effectiveness in their basic business of educating practitioners.

Practical Philosophy:
Political, Moral, Scientific

If it is done well, the process of liberal education will inevitably culminate in an acute awareness of ignorance. We teach the disciplines, our relatively settled methods of thought. But the further we go in our teachings, the more uncertain things are bound to seem. We reach the limits of reliable knowledge quickly. We then have to teach the argument, apprise students of our confusions and doubts. We shall have to teach that beyond those things we are relatively sure we are entitled to think in common, there are vast latitudes of distinctive interpretation and, thus, great areas in which there can be genuine, legitimate, unsettleable differences of point of view.

It is not good enough to simply leave matters hanging there. We really do have to teach students how best to proceed in the face of divided counsel. As I said earlier, the relativizing experience cannot be the ultimate aim of education. Rather, we bring students to the point of fundamental perplexity in order to open the questions of truth and appropriate action. If there are so many diverse interpretations, how shall we in fact represent the nature of the case? How shall we then proceed?

We really have more to say about such questions than we sometimes think we do. For the whole point of our liberal political theory, and our scientific rationalism, is to try to resolve differences. These are disciplines for dealing intelligently with diversity of perspective, for creating universals out of particulars, common understanding out of personal opinion.

Let us take each of these resources in turn. The issue of how best to proceed in the face of fundamental difference is intrinsically political, in the only important sense of that much abused term.

The aim of political philosophy, from Aristotle onward, has been to advise us on how to create ideas of common purpose and right conduct in the face of diverse perspective and opinion. Our own society is based on a particularly tough-minded version of that legacy of thought. Thus, classic liberal democratic political theory simply assumes that conflicts over purpose and meaning are inevitable, but that in recognizing this fact, we will be led, rationally, to accept certain norms and procedures as imperative to a life in common, norms and procedures that do not stipulate a purpose, but that provide a just procedure for arriving at common purpose. The basic understanding is that individuals must consent to policies that will be binding on them, and that this consent must be demonstrated through institutions of free expression and open debate, voluntary contract, rule of law, and democratic process.

Liberal democracy is basically a coping strategy. It assumes perversity, sustained discord in thought, in the operations of the mind, in the desires and demands of individuals, what they seek from the common life. It does not presume any dependable human capacity for rational convergence on a single point of view. It does not assume that we will all find, and affirm, a single truth, a single sense of the human good. Liberal democracy expresses, and attempts to come to grips with, the darker side of our nature, the perversity of our thought. Thus it is revealing to see liberal democracy in relation to the alternative method of resolving differences that has steadily accompanied it through all the ages, from Aristotle, through the Enlightenment, into our own times. That other method of conflict resolution is, of course, scientific inquiry. Here we account for the brighter side of our nature, the possibility that through deliberation, investigation, painstaking checking and rechecking, we might, just possibly, come to a common view of at least some things.

Like liberal democracy, scientific rationality is a means for trying to transform discord over purpose and meaning into common understanding. Again, it is assumed that this commonality must be reached through voluntary, informed consent. There must be open forums of expression and discourse, procedures that assure that no alternatives are excluded. There must be mechanisms for correcting existing error. But here—and the expectation is still astonishing no matter how many times it is stated—it is assumed that concurrence will be wrought by *finding a pattern of meaning or purpose that matches the order of meaning and purpose present in the nature of the world itself.*

These two methods of "conflict resolution" are the joint pillars that support all our efforts. Liberal democracy stands for the realist, scientific inquiry for the idealist, element in systematic thought. These disciplines of thought are interdependent and complementary, and we teach one to the exclusion of the other at great risk of totally mistaking the nature of our human capacity to arrive at rational meaning and rational order. Teach that concurrence can be won only by the accommodation and aggregation of individual standpoints, as the radical democrats do, and you foreclose the possibility that we might, in fact, have sound reason to come to agreement on the nature of things. Teach only that common assent should never be granted to anything short of demonstrable truth and you foreclose all of our opportunities for mutual tolerance, understanding, compromise, and getting on with the work at hand in the face of fundamental differences.

To learn to use these durable, well-established habits of mind at the fullest philosophic level is the obvious culmination of the process of liberal education. This is the goal we have been aiming at all along. Every step has been contrived to reach this end.

Our students now have mastered the fundamental disciplines of thought that we presume to represent the better paths of reason. They have come to comprehend the view of the universe, and humanity, that we currently endorse. They can now perform, and correct their own performance, in light of fundamental standards of best practice. They have begun to act as participants in the work of critical reason, the general, public process of appraisal of our collaborative methods of understanding and purposive action. They have been exposed to the relativizing experience that follows from the doubt, uncertainty, and ambiguity that lies at the end of the line of any method of reason. Now they learn what we know about how best to deal with confusion, conflict, puzzlement, and mutual incomprehension, in the name of achieving common purpose and common understanding. This is about as far as we can go. Beyond this point, there is little more that we are actually entitled to teach.

The Question for Critics

This is, as I say, a minimal program of reform in our notion of liberal education, one that would work efficiently to promote the cultivation of practical reason. Everything contained in the scheme is already taught. This program is well within the capabilities of existing disciplines. We need no new doctrine, no new knowledge, no new organization to put this into effect. Yet I am sure that this modest, almost excessively conventional, proposal will meet everywhere with vigorous dissent. We can ignore the criticism of those whose rarified specialties and idiosyncratic interests have not, in their own estimation, received sufficient recognition. The more serious objections will be philosophical and, I believe, ideological. They will be animated by a different conception of the fundamental purpose of liberal education. So let us begin the debate, here and now. Let those who would do otherwise present their own schema, and let them show how it satisfies our public expectations for the educational mission of the university, and how it is compatible with the university's own capabilities, how it represents what the university can teach with integrity.

CHAPTER EIGHT

The Governance of the University

The university exists to prescribe the life of the mind. It cannot, even if it wanted to, avoid making distinctions between the better and the worse habits of thought, for this is simply what universities do. It is inherent in their purpose. And the distinctive characteristic of these institutions leads us in the end to a straightforward question of political organization. How should decisions about what the university will and will not teach be made? And who should make them?

As I have said, the university has to justify its teachings. Its knowledge is public knowledge. But to whom, specifically, does it owe this justification? To say simply "to the public" is quite obviously not good enough. We have to be able to frame a clear picture in our minds of a political process that actually would be capable of deliberating and deciding issues of educational purpose and program. What then are the appropriate forums for the critical appraisal of the university's curriculum? And who is entitled to participate in these forums? Thus do we come to one of the oldest questions of political theory: Who are the guardians? And who is going to guard the guardians?

The official answer to these questions, of course, is that the specialists in the various disciplines decide what is worthy of being taught, and the faculty, as a body, are the trustees of the entire curriculum. But, as I have noted, such superintendence is more nominal than real. Except in the most egregious cases, it is clearly understood that no one asks impertinent questions about whether what others are teaching is sound, or worthwhile. If each leaves the other alone, then we can all do as we please. Further, it is generally assumed that there are no standards of truth, pertinence, or worth that apply across fields. So the faculty may have collegial responsibilities, but they do not constitute a *collegium*.

Political Theory and the University

We have to do better than this. But, unfortunately, there is very little guidance available in such matters. Political science, strangely, has rarely considered the governance of universities (or any institution other than the state for that matter). Today, political theory seems mainly intent on trying to state the ideal conditions of liberal democratic politics. Thus, a political system is regarded as in order to the extent that it rests on equality of voice and vote, if it is impartial among rival interests, does not stack the deck or prefigure the outcomes. A liberal democratic regime, it is said, must be neutral with regard to fundamental ideas of the public good.[1]

Thus, a good government should be equally open to all opinions and preferences, to all possibilities. In effect, as Jürgen Habermas puts it, politics should be a realm of "undistorted communication."[2] Each person must feel equally entitled, and qualified, to put forth opinions and policy options, to question and criticize the positions put forward by others. The process should be open to all possibilities, receptive to all challenges, even those which go to the foundation assumptions of the enterprise. (Should there be a state at all? Or a university?) No one should feel inhibited because of presumed differences in authority, status, or knowledge. There should be no limits on how a state of affairs may fairly be defined or construed, what implications may properly be drawn from a conception of the situation. Nothing, in short, should be out of bounds. Everything is open, on the table, and all are considered equally competent as participants.[3]

Such may be the ideal conditions of democracy. But is this the basis on which to found the government of the university? Granted, the university performs a public function and must justify its teaching. But does this mean that the "public," however it is construed, must be convinced, beyond a reasonable doubt, that the physics curriculum is in order as it stands? It is true that our systems of knowledge must be *completely* corrigible, that it should be possible to challenge root assumptions, to ask indeed whether we should even have a university, or a physics. But does this mean that we must be required to go back to first principles every time there is a challenge, every time a heckler suggests that the emperor is without clothes? Is it necessary to respond to every opinion that things might be done differently? Are we really prepared to say that all "preferences" about the university are to count precisely the same? Do we really want to endorse the bald utilitarian, or positivist, maxim that we cannot tell which views are better founded in deciding what we shall teach?

This may be the logic of ideal democracy, but it is not the path of practical reason, and, as I have suggested, practical reason seems essential to the success of liberal democratic politics.[4] In practical reason, we must first come to understand—and to master—the rationale for established forms of practice as a condition for participation in the enterprise in question. From this base, we may be able to go on to grasp the pattern, to develop the competence to critique prevailing standards against some larger idea of inherent purpose. In this way, we may come to *contribute* to the enterprise. In the historic order of the guild, the journeyman is presumed capable of carrying out the work with skill, but only the master is qualified to determine how the work is properly done. And for Peirce, of course, the test of reliable knowledge was concurrence within a community of *qualified* observers. The question of knowledge had nothing to do with public preference or public will.

It might very well be that liberal democratic citizenship similarly presupposes a certain skill, the mastery of certain disciplines of analysis and inquiry. The great political theorists did not in fact teach that liberal democratic politics could rest on raw opinion, anything that came to mind. The classic liberals—Hobbes, Locke, Hume, Kant, Mill—assumed that citizen competence required the cultivation of a certain state of mind, of enlightened self-interest, and they hardly thought that a spontaneous, widespread, or automatic disposition. The great democrats—Rousseau, Jefferson, and the like—also believed that government by the people required the development of a certain civic sense, a certain frame of mind.

Should we really expect civic competence to be universal? The democratic idealists—Dewey, Habermas, Dahl, Lindblom, and Barber—actually seem able to imagine a public composed entirely of competent citizens.[5] Others, most conspicuously Mill, have had their doubts.

The awkward part, of course, is that it is exceedingly hard to stipulate a test of civic competence. The minimum standards—literacy, constitutional knowledge—seem impertinent, in both senses of the word. But how identify the capacity for disinterested, shrewd, sound public judgment? Perhaps the quality is more situational than personal: it pops up in unexpected people, at unexpected times, a kind of sane responsibility under pressure, while those most expected to possess it may become craven, or lose their bearings.

It is hard for me to imagine a political order based on the expectation of equal competence for political reason among all citizens. I find it more sensible to differentiate two kinds of participation equally pertinent to political discourse. On the one hand, there is disinterested, practical deliberation on common problems. On the other, there is interested appeal, protest, remonstrance, criticism, and cries of pain. This is by far the more general form of political expression, and it is as essential to good governance as political reason itself, for there must be common awareness of hostility, outrage, and disappointment, of incompetence or acts of tyranny, great and small, on the part of those who govern.

As Aristotle said, it is the dweller, not the builder, who knows the value of the house, the diner, not the cook, who is the proper judge of the meal. The people know "where it pinches."[6] Still, it is the builder and the cook who must decide how to improve the house and the meal, and to find remedy for injury requires practical political judgment.

How does all this bear on the governance of universities?

As a political order, the university is unique in one very peculiar respect. It is the only polity I know that, as a natural result of its function, creates a constituency that, in principle, is qualified to judge its performance. The graduates of the university are members of the guild. Presumably, they are competent to participate, as citizens, in its affairs. There is, it would seem, a qualified public to which the university might answer.

Beyond this, of course, there is a larger public affected by the university's actions. Ideas have consequences. It is the very intent of the American university to critique and to try to improve the conditions of practice in every area of endeavor. It is pertinent then for the larger public to participate in the appraisal of the work of the university. The question is how to relate these two processes—these two publics—in a system of government that would generate the exercise of practical reason.

The Constitutional Question

The approach I have taken to the governance of universities follows directly from the line of argument of this book. The problem, first suggested in Chapter 3, is to reconcile the public and the intrinsic functions of the university. First we ask what we want the university to teach. Then we ask whether the university can teach this with integrity. The aim is to generate a process of practical reason that will work to resolve these questions.

This looks very much like a classic problem of constitutional design. The issue is to contrive checks and balances so that both the public interest, and the university's inherent interest, are effectively represented, but in which neither can prevail without the concurrence of the other. The object, as in James Madison's theory in crafting the United States Constitution, is both to prevent certain identifiable evils, and to require potentially rival factions to *deliberate,* to reason together about the best means for advancing the common cause.

The four perils we must contrive to avoid are these:

First, and most familiar, is the threat that the public will prevent the university from teaching something it deems worthy of being taught on the ground that it will endanger the social fabric, or morality. This is the classic issue of academic freedom, unchanged since Socrates was accused of corrupting the youth of Athens. My case, not uncontroversial, is that neither the public nor the faculty has the right to make this decision alone.

The second concern is that the public will require the teaching of subjects that the faculty regard as of dubious value, or beyond their competence. The charge may be to promote "right thinking" in politics, environmental ethics, or the marketing of shirts—the ideological salience matters not in the least. Or the issue may be to promote a program of research, of disciplined inquiry, into some urgent social issue, some promising technology, some commercial scheme. Again I say (and again I expect many to be uncomfortable with the thought) that such matters should not be decided by either the faculty or the public alone. The university, out of simple indifference, may neglect real possibilities for enhancing social intelligence and social performance, which, I have insisted throughout, is one of its avowed functions. However, the greater peril, I believe, is that the faculty will not resist dubious projects, for there are always academic operators only too eager to jerry-rig a science, and a curriculum, if the price is right.

The third peril is that the faculty will insist on teaching a doctrine that the public thinks intellectually unsound. This is not the case of teachings said to run against social convention. Here the question is how to respond to the charge that what the university teaches is not good literature, or not good science. What if evidence is adduced that the engineering curriculum is hopelessly out of date compared with foreign institutions? Or that the English department is teaching a particular mode of interpretation to the exclusion of obvious alternatives? Again, are we really satisfied that the faculty is entitled to be the final judge of this issue, that there is no public competent to address such questions?

The final case then is what to do in the face of the claim that the university excludes some valid body of knowledge, or some potentially important field of inquiry, from its program. This need not be merely a question of whether to teach creationism or parapsychology. It may also concern more serious questions, such as whether certain disciplines have defined their paradigms so narrowly as to exclude important areas of knowledge that would naturally fall within their domains. Again, should either faculty or laity be the ultimate judge of these issues?

The constitution of the university should attempt to prevent these corruptions. However, the equally compelling reason for constituting the university as a "mixed regime," in the tradition from Aristotle, is to create a forum for the exercise of practical reason. The aim is to structure a situation that will require reflexive deliberation on the purposes of the university.

The Search for a Forum for Practical Reason

How shall we go about doing this? How shall we introduce the appropriate measure of public involvement into the governance of the university? The obvious answers are none too appealing. We seem to have a choice between the appallingly dangerous and the totally innocuous. Our legacy of political forms, and theories, seems woefully inadequate to the matter at hand.

Does anyone imagine the performance of the public university would actually be *enhanced* were it made more closely subject to the authority of state legislatures? Should we hold hearings on the curriculum? Should we define educational priorities by legislative vote? There are more than enough pressures today for legislatures to exert control over public universities, usually in the name of economy and efficiency, as part of the general urge to seek out slack and waste in all public agencies. But this is not the balanced solution we seek. The university is not just another public agency. The object is not simply that the university become more responsive to public will. We do need to preserve, indeed to strengthen, that strange quasimedieval belief that the university is a kind of natural autonomous corporation which the state is obligated to nurture and protect but which must be permitted to define and seek its own ends. This little atavism in our public philosophy, this throwback to predemocratic, Aristotelian ways, is something to be cherished and relentlessly sustained. Else we lose all integrity.

The second thought that commonly comes to the fore when talk turns to expressing the public interest in the university is somehow to enhance the authority of the trustees. New schemes of representation and methods of management are bandied about. But we know there is little in such proposals. Whether in industry or education, boards of directors seldom actually change things in our society. They are there to keep the enterprise afloat, and protect appearances. Like most of the everyday proposals for revising the structure of faculty committees, and the relation of these to the administration, tinkering with the power of trustees is a form of busywork, a way of preoccupying oneself with the proper arrangement of the deck chairs on the *Titanic*. This is not how we are going to come to grips with fundamental questions of educational philosophy, and we know it.

Some, romantically, can imagine the university constituted as a kind of town meeting, with faculty, students, and the "community" somehow all engaged in the democratic deliberation of educational purpose. Frankly, I am far from sanguine about the prospects of such ventures. Too readily, such forums can be dominated by the intense, those with particular interests or specific agendas. Muddle and misunderstanding come easily. In the specific context of the university, one is apt to see, I suspect, either excessive deference to the faculty or a kind of bumptious arrogance concerning the presumptions of experts.

In any event, the faculty probably will, in the end, display their remarkable capacities to resist change. (It is said that reforming a curriculum is like trying to move a graveyard.) Pure democrats believe that if you give the people unrestricted capacity to debate and decide all will go well. Chastened democrats have no such illusions. My own view is that we need a very precise, subtle instrument if we are properly to deliberate the purposes of the university.

The best I can imagine would be a system of what I shall call simply Education Forums. I see these first as panels, created on each campus, composed of an equal number of faculty and alumni—as the public putatively best qualified to judge the institution's performance. Students have an important role to play in appraising the *present* program of the university: the quality of instruction, the suitability of services, and the like. But, by definition, they have no particular competence to make judgments on the *future* of the university. They have no perspective. They have "interests" that must be recognized, but they are not yet actually "citizens" of the enterprise.

The first function of the Forums might be to receive a report from the faculty justifying the present curriculum. Simply to get the faculty to make a clear statement of educational purpose would be a heroic accomplishment. But ideally, the Forum would go on to ask probing questions. A dialogue might be joined. A common sense of purpose and problem might emerge, and a search for solutions.

I have served on accreditation teams and review boards. I have few illusions. I know that most of these efforts would end in formality or in frustration. But in a few instances, things will jell. Some forums will find common ground. Here and there, new educational experiments will emerge and their merits will be debated elsewhere in the evolving network of such forums.

However, such forums organized only at the level of the college or university would not be sufficient. The campuses are hardly sovereign in educational matters. We say the faculty sets the curriculum. But normally the professors follow the doctrines of the learned professions, of the guilds. The fulcrum of change actually lies at a different level. The debate on educational philosophy and policy must be framed and prosecuted elsewhere in the system.

The Disciplines and the Graduate Schools

If we are actually to engage in critical deliberation upon the performance of the universities, we must do so at the level of the disciplines. But this raises a curious question about the political order of higher education. Where are the forums where we might consider the teachings of the various academic professions? The disciplines, after all, lead a shadowy existence. They are not truly incorporate. Their professional associations are little more than chambers of commerce, intended to hold meetings and bestow honors. The annual conventions advance careers, not knowledge. The institutions of the professions do not really decide things.

The actual locus of power over the curriculum lies in the major graduate schools—in the graduate departments. Jaroslav Pelikan, in his Carnegie Foundation report on graduate education of 1983, stated that "the graduate school finds itself in the role of the university's bureau of standards." He went on to argue, "There is no denying that when the graduate school's definition of scholarship makes its presence felt within the work of the college teacher, it can fundamentally distort the commitment of the undergraduate curriculum to the aims of liberal education." Thus, across the curriculum, it comes to be assumed that the undergraduate major should look like "a miniature graduate program."[7]

So let us imagine the institution of education forums in the leading graduate departments. I imagine these as composed equally of members of the graduate faculty and the specific public of the department and the discipline: practitioners, clients, employers—but on this occasion, particularly representatives of the teaching institutions.

None of this strikes me as a radical reform, a sharp break from existing ways. In fact, the idea of the education forums seems no more than an extension of a pattern of public participation in the life of the American university which has been present since the beginning.

In many applied fields, from medicine to forestry, city planning to accountancy, law to agriculture, there is a close, structured relationship between the academic disciplines and the organized communities of practitioners. We can think of this relationship as part of the overall organization, and the internal system of governance, of the profession or enterprise.[8] In such applied fields, the stipulation of best practice, the definition of the normative culture of the profession, the certification of practitioners, are functions performed through close, deliberative collaboration between academics and professionals. This relationship is also the focus of reflexive examination of prevailing doctrines. This is a forum for practical reason.

In the ideal conception of this relationship, the entire profession is constituted as a community of inquiry. In theory, the surgeon, like the scientific farmer or the practicing engineer, is supposed to be contributing to the development of knowledge in the field, through skeptical experiment and pragmatic examination of the results of following prescribed methods. There is an expected give-and-take between academic and practitioner. The relationships are porous and mutually reinforcing. The reconciliation of the public and intrinsic functions of education and inquiry does not imply the confrontation of rival constituencies. It is a common commitment.

Now it is often said that such guildlike arrangements actually impair critical reexamination of practice, that they insulate certain professions from public scrutiny and public responsibility. Up to a point, this is a worthwhile caution. One does want to insure that a wide range of views is represented, for without this, orthodoxy goes unchallenged and the puzzlement which is essential to practical reason cannot occur. Nonetheless, the assertion that all such relationships are bound to be captured by entrenched interests, that the terms of practice should be decided only by the bracing competitiveness of free markets or absolute responsiveness to public will, is no more than political ideology. The fashionable hostilities to all institutions that serve to reflect upon and establish practice simply leaves us without forums for practical reason.

Ideally, the system of education forums would recapitulate the process of practical reason itself. The first step is to make manifest the rationale for prevailing practice. Hence, in its initial justification of its pedagogy, the faculty is in effect "teaching" the councils why it has presumed to channel and nurture thought as it has. Then, in the examination of such statements, in the measurement of practice against implicit notions of purpose and possibility, critical reason begins.

From the confrontation of rival approaches within the discipline, and out of the presentation of public claims and concerns, we "teach the argument," undergo the relativizing experience of confronting diverse perspectives. This creates the classic pragmatic situation of perplexity. Now creative thinking, the process of conjecture and its critique, begins as the councils come to face the practical question of "what to do." The skills of scientific, moral, and political reason will have to be invoked to come to terms with the issue.

If all went well, a very broad array of prospective projects might arise from the process. Certain elements of existing practice would be found wanting. A variety of remedies would be proposed. Now the scene shifts to the local forums, the campus councils, who must ask, again, what practically ought to be done in their particular case. We might hope for diverse initiatives, some spreading to become general patterns, new conventions of educational purpose, for none of us want a world that is perpetually experimental. Let us hope also that the diverse colleges and universities would then press the graduate schools to adopt programs of inquiry and graduate training more appropriate to those emerging educational ideals.

Of Process and Substance

Now this is the best I can do. And I do not believe it is quite good enough. I do not believe we have resolved the question of how we can best go on from here.

What I have done is to take up the ancient exercise of the political scientist. I have tried to contrive an institution that would check and balance interests and thus induce a debate on the common good. I have tried to generate practical reason mechanically. It is as though I were trying to fashion a device to ignite an engine. To recommend a procedural artifice in politics is always dubious, conjectural. Such contrivances are not the final answer. They are, in the end, precisely that, an exercise.

Political scientists, of course, know that constitutional engineering is never enough. You can write an ideal constitution for a wretched, sullen country and it will do absolutely no good at all. On the other hand, when a people get caught up in a rich way of thinking, the institutions matter hardly at all. When the people see the point, catch on to the pattern, and the pattern, the philosophy, leads to a fine unfolding trail of possibilities for individual and common action, to challenging puzzles and predicaments, to opportunities to create and excel, then organization is spontaneous and automatic. Granted, you need constitutional principles to set the rules and the limits, to make sure that the large commitments to human rights, to basic humanity and political decency are upheld. But you do not need institutions to provoke deliberation. Set structures, official rigidities, are left behind. Purposive collaboration emerges on the strength of the idea. Thus it was in the early days of high-energy physics, commercial aviation, public health, and the Age of Exploration. You need settled systems mainly when the possibilities of a way of thinking begin to run dry and you want to keep the excitement, and the results, of the venture alive, though sometimes, to be sure, you can provoke new ideas by organizational contrivance and guile.

What is most important then is simply that we think consciously, publicly, about purpose, that we ask persistently about the point of our ventures, the aims of our major institutions. Might we not be better off in our pronouncements, our disputations, our commentaries, our interrogations of officials, candidates, and one another, if we asked insistently what it was that we expected the auto industry, the insurance business, the Forest Service, the authorities on urban problems to do?

Here we have concentrated on the university, that institution we single out to think through the meaning, significance, and point of events and actions. And by now it should be apparent that the logic, the ordering, the constitution of a disciplined deliberation is a system of government in itself. It is in *recognizing* that we need to reconcile our public expectations for what the university will teach with its inherent powers and purposes that we come to principles for its government, its political order. It does not work the other way around. Form follows function. The system of government does not determine our purposes. Our purposes determine the system of government. We have to take thought before we set up the committees! Is this not wondrous, unorthodox, counsel indeed?

Teaching and Research: Education and Inquiry

Such a vision of sustained deliberation upon the educational mission of the university is apt to upset what many take to be the natural order of things. The conventional understanding is that research comes before teaching. The university teaches what it has found out. This is, I think, why the university has spent so little time pondering its pedagogy. It takes that to be self-evident. The task of teaching is to communicate the fruits, and the methods, of research.

But if we were to start to ask seriously, systematically, publicly what we intend the process of education to accomplish, the matter would be different. The order which seems so natural would to a certain extent be reversed. Now the educational mission would define the agenda for research.

As matters now stand, research is thought to have a life of its own. The disciplines progress and unfold according to their own internal rhythms. Old theories are challenged by new, puzzles arise, new discoveries have to be assimilated to doctrine. The process is presumed to be driven by no purpose other than inquiry, than the enhancement of understanding itself.

If we actually tried to think through, and decide, what education should accomplish in the mind and heart of the student, however, matters might be different. If we really wanted to *enhance* the life of the mind, we might proceed differently. We might want our professors of English to write more poetry and less criticism. We might wish our scientists to wonder more and pay less attention to technical minutiae. And if we really *did* decide that we wanted to teach best practice, the discernment of excellence and error, then we might want to charge our social scientists and philosophers with finding out how our human capacity for judgment works.

So however we organize the process, the question to be asked in our deliberations on the university is simply: Where do we go from here? We have learned, so far, to do some wondrous things with the curiously personal, curiously social, power of organized thought, with that propensity of ours to spin out ideas, test them, check and challenge them, change them, channel them to particular purposes. Thus have we made mathematics and hybrid corn, international law and opinion polling, organ transplants and theology.

If we think about it aright, I think we will come to realize that we are still quite new at this entire game. There is so much we haven't tried yet. So what will it be? Do we want to teach people to think more intelligently about public purpose when they act as citizens? Then we must try to find out what *does* happen, and what *should* happen, in various forums of deliberation, from the Socratic dialogue to the politics of large democratic nations. Do we want people to learn to live more in harmony with nature so as to sustain the resources and the beauties of the earth? In that case, we'd better start finding out more about our peculiar place in the order of life for, sanctimonious ecological pronouncements notwithstanding, we really have no clear idea of what "living in accord with nature" actually means. Do we need better scientists and engineers? Then we must start imagining where there might be patterns in the order of matter, in the world out there, that we now hardly suspect exist, that we have barely begun to probe and ponder. Do we need better teachers? Then we'd best think more about the mystery of teaching and learning, what it means to catch on, and to be able to go on, to discern the pattern that presumably all can learn to see. Do we even want to teach integrity, character, morality? Then we are going to have to think squarely, seriously, systematically, about what we *mean* by good and evil, and probably to our great profit, we should try to learn more about the peculiar human capabilities of responsibility, cooperation, steadfastness, and love.

The list is unending, inviting, and obviously daunting. It certainly challenges some familiar notions about what research is all about. But everything we can claim to teach with integrity we must at least *partially* understand. And when we examine the kind of knowledge that is presupposed by some of the things we most desperately want to teach, we see quite clearly where we have to go from here. Right over the brink. Right out into regions we have hardly begun to fathom and where we have been confidently told we must not presume to go. But this is precisely how matters stand. The questions that most concern us now, the things we most earnestly want people to understand, lie beyond the line we have been taught defines the boundary of the known and the knowable. So we really do have to work up our courage and venture out.

This is all a little scary, and we are tempted to settle for the tried and true, to obey the familiar strictures. But we have been *led* here precisely by those strictures, by the entire force of that science and philosophy that do give meaning to our life and work, and that insist also that we keep checking and challenging, looking for pattern, for something that better satisfies our vague yearning to understand where we are and what we are intended to do.

To be sure, it is not in our power to overcome our final sense of "strangeness" in the world. That move is up to God. But, in the meantime, there is no reason to be too reluctant, too unassuming, about just how much we might come to understand. Nor is there any reason to suppose that what we find in unknown regions will be dangerous or frightening. It might just as well be comforting. We really do not know just how late it is, and we have absolutely no way of telling just how far we are from home.

Notes

Index

Notes

Chapter One: Liberal Education and Practical Reason

1. Eva T. H. Brann, *Paradoxes of Education in a Republic* (Chicago: University of Chicago Press, 1979), 89–93.

2. Lawrence Veysey, *The Emergence of the American University* (Chicago: University of Chicago Press, 1965).

3. On the tribulations of such programs, see Richard M. Jones and Barbara Leigh Smith, *Against the Current: Reform and Experimentation in Higher Education* (Cambridge: Schenkman, 1984).

4. William James, *Pragmatism* (New York: Longmans, 1907). On the nature of philosophical pragmatism generally, see H. S. Thayer, *Meaning and Action* (New York: Bobbs-Merrill, 1968); John E. Smith, *Purpose and Thought* (Chicago: University of Chicago Press, 1978); Sandra B. Rosenthal, *Speculative Pragmatism* (La Salle, Ill.: Open Court, 1986). On Peirce, see Eugene Freeman, ed., *The Relevance of Charles Peirce* (La Salle, Ill.: Hegelier Institute, 1983). In present context, see particularly: Charles Sanders Peirce, "The Fixation of Belief," and "How to Make Our Ideas Clear," both in Justus Buchler, ed., *The Philosophical Writings of Peirce* (New York: Dover, 1955), 5–41.

5. Karl Popper, *The Logic of Scientific Discovery* (New York: Harper, 1968), 34–39.

6. Jürgen Habermas, *The Theory of Communicative Competence*, trans. T. McCarthy (Boston: Beacon Press, 1981). The best guide to the difficult writings of Habermas is Thomas McCarthy, *The Critical Theory of Jürgen Habermas* (Cambridge: MIT Press, 1978).

163

7. Clark Kerr, *The Uses of the University* (Cambridge: Harvard University Press, 1982).

8. David Braybrooke and Charles E. Lindblom, *A Strategy of Decision* (New York: Free Press, 1963), 147–54.

Chapter Two: The Rationale of the Going Concern

1. On Hayek's view of spontaneous order, see particularly John Gray, *Hayek on Liberty* (New York: Blackwell, 1984), 27–55. For Dewey, see *The Public and Its Problems* (New York: Holt, 1927), 143–232, and of the many fine commentaries, see particularly Rosenthal, *Speculative Pragmatism* 147–94.

2. Karl Popper, *The Logic of Scientific Discovery*. See also Imre Lakatos, "Falsification and the Methodology of Scientific Research Programmes," in Imre Lakatos and Alan Musgrave, eds., *Criticism and the Growth of Knowledge* (New York: Cambridge University Press, 1970), 91–196.

3. This idealist strand is most apparent in Peirce and Royce but it is also evident in James and Dewey. It is an idea that is in the air in the formative years of the American university. See Daniel J. Wilson, *Science, Community and the Transformation of American Philosophy: 1860–1930* (Chicago: University of Chicago Press, 1990), 40–55. See also John E. Smith, *Purpose and Thought* (Chicago: University of Chicago Press, 1978), 119–94.

4. Gerald Graff, *Professing Literature* (Chicago: University of Chicago Press, 1987), 65.

5. Wilson, *Science, Community and the Transformation of American Philosophy*. A similar tale is told in David M. Ricci, *The Tragedy of American Political Science* (New Haven: Yale University Press, 1984), 3–28.

6. Jürgen Herbst, *The German Historical School in American Scholarship* (Ithaca: Cornell University Press, 1965), 25.

7. Cited in Robert Ulich, "Philosophy of Education," in Charles Frankel, ed., *Issues in University Education* (New York: Harper, 1959), 31.

8. Hannah Arendt even supposes that human judgment, the appraisal of performance, pertains to the spectators, not the actors. But then, Arendt supposed that human action is generally to be regarded as spectacle. See particularly *The Life of the Mind* (New York: Harcourt, 1978).

9. Wilson, *Science, Community and the Transformation of American Philosophy* 121–49.

10. Smith, *Purpose and Thought;* Rosenthal, *Speculative Pragmatism.*

11. Richard Rorty, *Contingency, Irony and Solidarity* (New York: Cambridge University Press, 1989).

Chapter Three: Purpose

1. One distinguished scholar who seems to think this way is Amy Guttman, *Democratic Education* (Princeton: Princeton University Press, 1987).

2. See E. D. Hirsch, Jr., *Cultural Literacy* (Boston: Houghton Mifflin, 1987).

3. The prominent exponents of this position in contemporary philosophy include Alasdair MacIntyre, *After Virtue* (Notre Dame, Ind.: Notre Dame University Press, 1981), and Michael Walzer, *Spheres of Justice* (New York: Basic Books, 1983), 3–30, 312–22.

4. For various conceptions of education for citizenship, see Brann, *Paradoxes of Education in a Republic;* Martin S. Dworkin, ed., *Dewey on Education* (New York: Teachers College, Columbia University, 1959); Alexander Meiklejohn, *The Experimental College,* ed. J. W. Powell (Cabin John, Md.: Seven Locks Press, 1981); Guttman, *Democratic Education.*

5. Charles E. Lindblom, *Inquiry and Change* (New Haven: Yale University Press, 1990), 59–134.

6. On pure democracy, see Benjamin Barber, *Strong Democracy* (Berkeley: University of California Press, 1981), and Carole Pateman, *Participation and Democratic Theory* (New York: Cambridge University Press, 1970). On civic republicanism, see William M. Sullivan, *Reconstructing Public Philosophy* (Berkeley: University of California Press, 1982).

7. Robert Bellah et al., *Habits of the Heart* (Berkeley: University of California Press, 1985).

8. An excellent example is Thomas A. Spragens, Jr., *Reason and Democracy* (Durham: Duke University Press, 1990).

9. Habermas, *Theory of Communicative Competence,* and McCarthy, *The Critical Theory of Jürgen Habermas.*

10. In addition to Spragens, *Reason and Democracy,* see Stephen Salkever, *Finding the Mean* (Princeton: Princeton University Press, 1989).

11. Ernest L. Boyer, *College: The Undergraduate Experience* (New York: Harper, 1982), 12, 13, 110.

12. On the centrality of utility in American higher education philosophy, see Veysey, *Emergence of the American University,* and Brann, *Paradoxes of Education in a Republic.*

13. One very clear statement of a credo that liberal education should be pursued for its own sake appears in J. M. Cameron, *On the Idea of a University* (Toronto: University of Toronto Press, 1978), 9.

14. On the practical character of liberal education, see John Henry Cardinal Newman, *On the Idea of a University* (1872; Notre Dame, Ind.:

Notre Dame University Press, 1982), 74–135. For a splendid reexamination of Newman, see Jaroslav Pelikan, *The Idea of the University: A Reexamination* (New Haven: Yale University Press, 1992).

15. I have in mind something like Lynne V. Cheney, *50 Hours* (Washington: National Endowment for the Humanities, 1989).

16. A very nice statement of Aristotle's philosophy of character and practical reason is found in Spragens, *Reason and Democracy* 23.

17. This is also a central theme in Allan Bloom, *The Closing of the American Mind* (New York: Simon and Schuster, 1987).

18. Rorty, *Contingency, Irony and Solidarity.*

Chapter Four: Competence

1. S. I. Benn and R. S. Peters, *Social Principles and the Democratic State* (London: George Allen and Unwin, 1959), 14–32; Charles W. Anderson, *Pragmatic Liberalism* (Chicago: University of Chicago Press, 1990), 1–13.

2. John W. Ziman, *Public Knowledge* (New York: Cambridge University Press, 1969).

3. Charles Sanders Peirce, "Fallibilism," *Philosophical Writings of Peirce* 42–59.

4. Popper, *Logic of Scientific Discovery.*

5. For a clear summary, see Spragens, *Reason and Democracy* 57–111. Other pertinent treatments are: Stephen Toulmin, *Human Understanding I* (Princeton: Princeton University Press, 1972); W. V. Quine, *From a Logical Point of View* (New York: Harper, 1953); Lakatos and Musgrave, *Criticism and the Growth of Knowledge;* Larry Laudan, *Science and Values* (Berkeley: University of California Press, 1984).

6. Graff, *Professing Literature* 144–60.

7. Annie Dillard, *Living by Fiction* (New York: Harper, 1983), 54.

8. Juliana Hunt, "Beyond The Ism." Manuscript.

9. Timothy Fuller, *The Voice of Liberal Learning: Michael Oakeshott on Education* (New Haven: Yale University Press, 1989).

10. Rorty, *Contingency, Irony and Solidarity* 19.

11. Peter L. Berger and Thomas Luckmann, *The Social Construction of Reality* (New York: Doubleday, 1967).

12. Paul K. Feyerabend, *Against Method* (London: Verso, 1975).

13. C. Fred Alford, "Epistemological Relativism and Political Theory: The Case of Paul K. Feyerabend," *Polity* 18 (Winter 1985): 204–23.

14. Feyerabend, *Against Method* 21–22.

15. A good example, although one with which I have some sympathy given the discipline in question, is Donald N. McClosky, *The Rhetoric of Economics* (Madison: University of Wisconsin Press, 1985).

16. John Kenneth Galbraith, *Economics, Peace and Laughter* (Boston: Houghton Mifflin, 1972), 269.

17. Robert M. Hutchins, *The Higher Learning in America* (New Haven: Yale University Press, 1936), 18.

18. Newman, *Idea of the University*.

19. Ibid. 100.

20. Ibid. 103.

21. Ibid. 105.

22. Hutchins, *Higher Learning in America* 66.

23. Ibid. 77–106.

24. Here I am simply generalizing Alasdair MacIntyre's point that moral philosophy makes little sense unless seen in relation to the Aristotelian tradition (*After Virtue*).

Chapter Five: Efficiency

1. R. S. Peters, *The Concept of Education* (London: Routledge and Kegan Paul, 1973), 27, 28, 31, 35.

2. Stephen Toulmin, *Foresight and Understanding* (New York: Harper, 1971), 55–59. I should note that my point in this section is generally consistent with Michael Polanyi, *Personal Knowledge* (New York: Harper, 1964).

3. Alfred North Whitehead, *The Aims of Education* (New York: Macmillan, 1929), 30–31.

4. Ludwig Wittgenstein, *Philosophical Investigations,* trans. G. E. M. Anscombe (New York: Macmillan, 1963), 59.

5. Ibid. 59–60.

6. W. W. Bartley III, *Unfathomed Knowledge, Unmeasured Wealth* (La Salle, Ill.: Open Court, 1990), 31–56.

7. John Dewey, *Experience and Nature* (New York: Norton, 1929), 212, 217.

8. Edward Lueders, *The Clam Lake Papers* (Nashville: Abingdon, 1977), 68.

9. William B. Drees, *Beyond the Big Bang* (La Salle, Ill.: Open Court, 1990).

10. Edmond Cahn, *The Sense of Injustice* (Bloomington: Indiana University Press, 1949).

Chapter Six: The Cultivation of Practical Reason

1. The most recent is Habermas. See McCarthy, *Critical Theory of Jürgen Habermas* 16–46. Aristotle's views may in fact have been closer to those propounded here. See Stephen Salkever, *Finding the Mean* (Princeton: Princeton University Press, 1990), 101.

2. Hutchins, *Higher Learning in America* 33–46.

3. I know I should be citing learned authority from educational psychology at this point. However, having poured over many tomes and studies, I find little that is precisely pertinent to my point. I think these views are generally consistent with what is known about human intellectual development, and I stand open to well-founded criticism and correction.

4. This tale has been told in many places. My favorite is Karl Polanyi, *The Great Transformation* (Boston: Beacon, 1944).

5. Here see particularly Thomas Kuhn, *The Copernican Revolution* (Cambridge: Harvard University Press, 1957), and Stephen Toulmin and June Goodspeed, *The Fabric of the Heavens* (New York: Harper, 1967).

6. I discuss this in much greater detail in *Pragmatic Liberalism*.

7. Smith, *Purpose and Thought* 58.

8. Allan Janik and Stephen Toulmin, *Wittgenstein's Vienna* (New York: Simon and Schuster, 1973), 202–38.

9. Werner Heisenberg, *Physics and Beyond* (New York: Harper, 1971), 82–92, 99, 215.

Chapter Seven: The Core of the Curriculum

1. C. P. Snow, *The Two Cultures and the Scientific Revolution* (New York: Cambridge University Press, 1979).

2. Alasdair MacIntyre, *Three Rival Versions of Moral Enquiry: Encyclopedia, Genealogy, and Tradition* (Indianapolis, University of Notre Dame Press, 1990).

3. See, for example, Robert E. Allison, ed., *Understanding the Chinese Mind* (New York: Oxford University Press, 1989).

4. Lorraine Code, *Epistemic Responsibility* (Hanover, N.H.: University Press of New England, 1987), 128–97.

5. John S. Rigdon and Sheila Tobias, "Too Often, College-Level Science Is Dull as Well as Difficult," *Chronicle of Higher Education,* March 27, 1991, A52.

6. John Rawls, *A Theory of Justice* (Cambridge: Harvard University Press, 1971), 395–449.

7. Dillard, *Living by Fiction* 170.

8. Karl Popper, *Conjectures and Refutations* (New York: Harper, 1965).

9. Heisenberg, *Physics and Beyond* 210.

Chapter Eight: The Governance of the University

1. On the idea of liberal neutrality, see particularly Rawls, *Theory of Justice* 395–450; Bruce Ackerman, *Social Justice in the Liberal State* (New Haven: Yale University Press, 1980); Ronald Dworkin, "Liberalism," in

Stuart Hampshire, ed., *Public and Private Morality* (New York: Cambridge University Press, 1978), 125–39. See also the critical review and response in William Galston, *Liberal Purposes* (New York: Cambridge University Press, 1991), 79–117.

2. Habermas, *Theory of Communicative Competence*.

3. On the ideal requirements of democracy, see Robert A. Dahl, *Democracy and Its Critics* (New Haven: Yale University Press, 1989), 106–31.

4. Spragens, *Reason and Democracy*.

5. Barber, *Strong Democracy;* Dahl, *Democracy and Its Critics;* Spragens, *Reason and Democracy;* Pateman, *Participation and Democratic Theory;* Lindblom, *Inquiry and Change*.

6. Aristotle, *The Politics,* trans. and ed. Ernest Barker (New York: Oxford University Press, 1974), 126.

7. Jaroslav Pelikan, *Scholarship and Its Survival* (New York: Carnegie Foundation for the Advancement of Teaching, 1983), 12–13.

8. For further discussion, see Anderson, *Pragmatic Liberalism* 45–55, 81–100.

Index